Glo-o-
What A Faith Journey

Near to the Heart of God Ministries

"This poor man cried, and the LORD heard him, and saved him out of all his troubles." Psalms 34:6

Bishop W.L. Bryant

UWriteit Publishing Company
Goldsboro, NC USA
www.uwriteitpublishingcompany.com
www.neartotheheartofgodmin.org

Glo-o-ory!!! What A Faith Journey by Bishop W.L. Bryant

ISBN: **ISBN-13: 978-0615746609 (UWriteIt Publishing Company)**
ISBN-10: 0615746608

First Printing January – 2013

Unless otherwise indicated, Scripture quotations in this book are from the King James Version of the Bible.

This publication is designed to provide information in regard to the subject matter covered. It is published with the understanding that the authors are not engaged in rendering legal counsel or other professional services. If legal advice or other professional advice is required, the services of a professional person should be sought.

Printed in the U.S.A.

Dedication

I am eternally grateful to God. I have been humbled and humiliated yet I will not complain. I have been transformed by GOD to new heights and depths in HIM. I love God with my whole heart.

I dedicate this ministry of serving Him and I thank Him for leading, guiding, and protecting me. God! Thank you for choosing me for these blessing...

- Blessing me with divine wisdom to educate others to address the needs of the homeless with the Word of God, and with love and compassion. To GOD BE THE GLORY!
- Blessing me with FAITH at a level I never could imagine that makes trusting and obeying HIM easy. To GOD BE THE GLOORY!!
- Blessing me with His most precious gift **LOVE!!!** in the person of Pastor Anita Flores-Bryant my wife and best friend and awesome tag team partner. To GOD BE THE GLOOORY!!!

Knee Knee thank you for your patience with me. I want to thank you Pastor Bryant for your obedience to God, your faith in God and your faithfulness to God. You have strengthened me daily even when I felt I had let us down.

We thank God for H. Saeda, and Aneida our amour bearers. I thank God for allowing us to have been blessed by Pastor Gladys for her prayers and blessings and the instrument in allowing us to be introduced to Chief Apostle Frank Bowden. Thank God for the Voice of Victory prayer line and all the prayer warriors that has been keeping us lifted up daily and helping us to blossom under the anointing of God. Amen, Great big Amen.

Prayer warriors remember all we have is faith!!!
TO GOD BE THE GLOOORY!!!

PREFACE

Often we hear the voice of God, and we pretend we didn't hear anything. Just imagine you are told to leave everything, and go on a homeless journey. Leaving all the luxuries and comforts of home behind to be homeless for a year. That's right, H-*O-M-E-L-E-S-S*. You are told to take nothing with you, but the clothes on your back I mean nothing. No credit cards, checks, passbook savings, no drivers license, Social Security card, no ID, and no cash. NOTHING!!! That's right take nothing but *F-A-I-T-H!!!* I had to obey God and walk with the homeless. *WHOW!!!*

What a *Journey*!

Now, you are told by the Lord to go, to different geographical locations to see how the needs of the homeless are met. Everything you have need of, will be provided for you. Ask no one for anything. Tell no one you are a minister. Take no job for wages until God releases you.

I've always had a burden in my heart for the homeless, and tried to recruit others in this worthy ministry. I have gone to other ministers, and asked them to team up with me. Only to get responses, such as: "That's a good work; I'll pray for you;' 'the

Lord, didn't call me to that work;' and 'I don't believe the Lord wants to force Himself on anyone;' 'let them come to Church, and then we help them."

I tell you what. Come on, I'll take you on a journey with me. Don't worry, you don't have to be afraid, as I was when I obeyed God and went with Him. You don't have to leave the comforts of your home. All I want you to do is keep an open mind and remember all we have is F-A-I-T-H!!! After going on this journey, I pray your heart and actions towards the homeless will make you realize, you too could wind up in a state of homelessness. Most Americans are living from paycheck to paycheck, and are only one paycheck away from homelessness.

I have always imagined the homeless as bums, alcoholics, drug addicts, or mentally ill. I have come to understand that homelessness is not prejudiced in any way. All I know is all the homeless have one thing in common; *ALL HOMELESS ARE A CREATION OF THE CREATOR!!! CAST YOUR CARES!!! ENJOY THE TRIP!!!*

The Purpose of This Book

This book is to be used to open the hearts, minds, and eyes to a problem that we see every day, and we try to sweep under the rug. It will also help us to deal with the needs of the homeless with love, compassion, and wisdom.

I observed some of the people that were serving in the soup kitchens. I would constantly ask the question. "Why are they serving?" Some would not have a smile, and at times would complain about serving the homeless. Then I began to realize, not all people that are in a church which served in this capacity were saved (had given their lives to God or accepted Jesus as their personal Savior). Only a foolish person will look for the attributes of Jesus in a person that does not know Him.

I greeted the servers many times as a homeless person only to be ignored more than to be responded to. Sometimes when I was greeted, there was no eye to eye contact. Serving the homeless is more than putting soup in a bowl and giving someone a sandwich and something sweet. Often times the homeless wanted a warm smile, or even a simple hug or handshake. I know the people had to serve the meals as quickly as possible. Some did this while thinking how quickly they could drive home to watch their TV's. Some complain about how smelly these people were that came to their church to eat.

Others complain about being on the committee in the first place.

Many times I heard nothing from the Bible or about Jesus during these soup kitchen meals. Often times the only indication that God was part of the occasion, was a simple grace, or blessing over the food. Every now and then, I would hear some hot testimony of what God had done for someone that was homeless. (I mean I heard testimonies of people getting jobs, and apartments after people that were hosting would pray for them and get them SAVED. Unfortunately, I would not see or hear any response from the people that were hosting the feeding). Not even an "Amen."

Because of rules, some places didn't allow preaching or even reading the Bible. It's easy to get caught up in our immediate busyness or jobs, and we fail to show ourselves friendly in order to make friends. I had to constantly ask the question: "**What Would Jesus do?**"

CHAPTER ONE

"Make me to go in the path of thy commandments; for therein do I delight." Psalms 119:35

I was in the pallet business. Now for the first time in ten years I couldn't sell a pallet. I called every pallet company I had dealt with in the past, but I couldn't get rid of any. Not even for half price.

While I lived and was a Pastor in Henderson, NC I had been working with other ministries that had been trying to do something for the homeless and the poor. I had invited some of the Churches to come together to feed the poor. Besides sharing the vision I had, of helping the poor and homeless, I also shared a vision of outreach to the abused, bruised, and battered women.

I began to hear overwhelming responses (or were they excuses?)

- "That's a great work; I'll pray for you";
- "The Lord didn't call me to that work"; and
- "The Lord don't force himself on anyone; let them come to the Church and then we can help them."

It's difficult to **understand how; we are going to get the homeless to Church if we make no effort to invite them.** This would sink deeper in my spirit whenever I would lead revivals and visit other cities only to see masses of people ask for money to buy something to eat. The response I heard most from church people was to tell them to stop begging. My heart was aching and broken; as I would see people give and instruct them not to buy drugs, alcohol, or cigarettes with that money.

Fed up with what was going on in North Carolina, I decided to sell some pallets to friends and businesses in Norfolk, VA. When I arrived in Norfolk I found that my friend was going out of the pallet business. I took the ride primarily to clear my mind of the sudden change in business.

After talking with a close friend, I thought I was out of the will of God. Perhaps I must have missed an assignment or God was trying to get my attention. **God was calling my number and because of my caller ID, He blocked the number!** I didn't know who was calling so I didn't answer. You know those private and unknown numbers. I soon left Norfolk and traveled to this paper plant in Virginia Beach to sell the load of pallets there. Even though they paid me for the pallets, they had sufficient supply and wouldn't buy anymore at that time.

Since I had a revival scheduled for Ahoskie, NC two weeks away, I offered to take pallets to this pallet company in Ahoskie for David my friend. I took a load a day the first week. I really wanted to haul two loads a day; but because of the grading system for the pallets, David wanted to send the best pallets to maximize his money. He was not prepared for me to haul as many as I desired, so I left the trailer in Virginia. I returned to my motel in North Carolina to rest for the weekend and to prepare for the Church, where I was going to run the revival.

Everybody was glad to see me Sunday morning, and we had Church! At the end of the service, the Pastor came to me to tell me the Lord must have sent me there, because he was trying to remember to call my secretary and tell her the revival was canceled. The smile he had on his face was something else. I didn't know if it was because he was glad I came, or that the revival was canceled. He didn't give me any reason why it was canceled. My heart was broken because the youth really looked forward to me coming.

Everything I had done seemed to be ineffective. Either God was trying to get my undivided attention, or He was mad at me. I went back to the motel to rest. Around 6:30 a.m. Monday morning I finished my prayer, and went to Virginia to pick up my trailer, and the first load. I arrived in North Carolina around 9:30 a.m., unloaded and headed back to Norfolk to pick up my second load by 10:00 a.m. I was heading back to North Carolina by noon. Look at God! About 1:00 p.m. I was about twenty minutes from the pallet yard and the engine blew. I was about an hour away, if I had to walk and no one decided to stop and give me a ride.

I walked to the diner right up the street to get

something to eat. When I finished, I went back to the truck. I raised the hood and this wrecker pulled up. My spirit picked up the owner and driver of the wrecker was a back-slidden preacher. I agreed to his services since he lived in route to the pallet yard and it was too late to unload, he took my truck to his house until the next morning then he dropped me off at the motel.

The next morning he came to the motel with the truck, and we went to the pallet yard. I spoke to the yardman and management and told them what had happened, asking if I could change the motor there. By lunch time I had the motor out. After a trip to the junkyard, (excuse me the used auto part yard) we had the forklift driver unload the new motor and place it in the truck. I hooked up the motor which started right up! I called it a night. Look at God!

Right after I hooked up, I met this young fireball of a man. This brother was on fire for the Lord. He rode pass me and then turned around in the middle of the road when he noticed my hood up. I was exhausted. He came up and greeted me with a great big hug, a warm smile and a very firm handshake. Never mind he was a brother of different skin pigmentation, short, well built, young and energetic. He greeted me with a very firm handshake, but he couldn't look me in my eyes. He then said, "Praise the Lord! Brother, Praise the Lord!" I could not believe the authority in his voice. I couldn't help but say "Praise Him; Praise Him!"

He asked me if he could give me a tract about Jesus. I accepted it, and for some reason I had to keep quiet about who I was and that I was saved. I was compelled to listen to him without interrupting. (Anyone that knows me knows that is quite difficult for me, not to interrupt. That's not me. Not as much as I have been known to talk.)

This brother tried to introduce me to Jesus without giving me a chance to get a word in, or respond to what he was saying. It was the same as an insurance salesman that would not take no for the answer. When this brother finished talking about Jesus; you would want to know Him if you already didn't. He gave me his testimony of how he met Jesus, how some lady put some grease all on top of his head, and she said a few words of prayer while she had her hand on his head; he hit the floor. Later he couldn't remember anything; but he knew for sure that he was not the same when he stood up. He wanted to give me a tract, and tell everybody he came in contact with about Jesus. He talked for 45 minutes. Then he decided to ask me if my truck was running, gave me his name as Nicholas.

I started the truck and told him I had to finish tightening up some loose ends. So I had to leave the truck overnight. I needed a ride to the motel. He took me to dinner. I knew right away I was in trouble and wasn't about to shake him until I was ready to leave town. He told me he had to help me, but he didn't know why. I didn't know whether or not to accept his help.

We decided to partake at an "all you care to consume" buffet as I always like to call them. At the dinner buffet we began to talk. The Lord began to reveal this man's personal business, so that I could minister to him. Because it was so personal I was hearing some deep terrible secrets. I wasn't use to ministering this way. God used me to even help him get healed of his prejudice, and his broken heart. Even with his wife about to divorce him, and take the kids, he was still praising the Lord.

We arrived at my motel, but I still didn't reveal to him that I was a minister. That was done by the owner of the motel when he greeted us because he called me Pastor Bryant, and gave me a praise report of what God had done as a result of a prayer request. My new brother was really surprised that he had come to the aid of a man of God. He paid for the room then told me he would see me in the morning to go to breakfast. I told him I always get up around 5:30 a.m. because I had to prepare myself for the day and for 6:00 a.m. prayer. He asked me to pray for him and his family before he left. We prayed, he left then I went to bed.

About 5:50 a.m. I heard a car pulling up in front of my room door. I couldn't help but think it was the fireball. **He greeted me with a great big smile on his face and he told me he had the best sleep and rest he had in a long time.** I asked him if he wanted to join me for prayer. Then I thought; that this was a time of intimacy between the Lord and me. I was doing things I hadn't normally done. It felt funny praying out loud for that first prayer of the day. Something was going on that I couldn't explain. For years my first prayer of the day was always in silence because I always had a thing about that being a secret prayer.

We went to breakfast then he dropped me back off at the truck. The foreman at the pallet yard was glad to see me because he had gotten in trouble for allowing me to work on the truck there. I told him all I had to do was to tighten up some loose ends. He was glad for me. I started the truck and let it run for about twenty minutes. Then I went to the auto parts store to get oil, filter, spark plugs and a few other items. When I returned I was happy everything was finished. I thanked everyone and tried to restart the truck. For some unknown reason it wouldn't start. I was through fooling with that truck!!!

I took a looooong walk. I walked and had a little talk with Jesus about my struggles (as if He didn't know). I pleaded with Him to reveal what it was He wanted me to do. God's prophetic anointing was stronger upon my life than I had experienced in a long time. It was so powerful that I was out of focus in my mind. God took me back to three different places: that place when I was first anointed to sing, then to where He first anointed me to preach, finally when He saved me.

God took me back to where I was first anointed to

sing to remind me of the healing that would come forth when I sang. This healing was not only for me but also for the persons that the songs ministered to. So I can now see that God had to take me back to the beginning to make me appreciate where He first anointed me to preach to make me remember **HIS GRACE. Oh! Look out MERCY; that's what HE had when He saved me. I was one of those people that was gifted and then saved.**

I was really charged up and now like Nicholas, going nowhere fast. I returned to that old truck and began praying for another motor, when someone drove up to offer me a car free of charge. I went with them to pick up the car, and drove the car back to where the truck was. **That was a quick answer to my prayer. Look at God!!!**

Well, it was already Friday and I didn't want to fool with the truck anymore. I was invited to preach at a church I knew nothing about so I began to prepare for Sunday service. I got back to the motel after Nicholas picked me up with his two sons. I went to the desk to pay for my room but it was taken care of and an envelope with money in it was waiting too. My room was paid in full for five days. I didn't have to pay anymore until Thursday Thanksgiving day. Look at God!!!

We went to my favorite rib and chicken spot. I felt a visitation from the Lord and thought something was about to happen. For some reason things that I was doing for others was now happening to me. I began to see God taking my faith level to the top, fine-tuning my ears, getting me ready for something.

I returned to the motel, showered, read a few scriptures then dosed off. I slept as if I didn't have a care in the world. I got up and had my prayer then went to breakfast. I saw the preacher that towed me to the pallet yard. I told him I was taking that motor out on Monday, that he could have that car and the two junk motors for scrap. He was glad, but could not understand why I was having so many problems. I was bragging about how quick God answered my prayer for another motor. I called my son in law and told him to bring me my Cadillac from Henderson, to meet me in Ahoskie. He came then I realized that he could not get back home unless he drove something. I took him to the truck where we took out all of the important items and papers, and then I sent him back to Henderson telling him to come back on Tuesday evening.

I spent a whole day with the spirit of gratitude and praise. Thanking God from where He had brought me. I opened my Bible to I Kings Chapter 13 reading it not once but three times. My ears began to burn, as they were being fine tuned to the whisper of His voice. I stopped worrying about the truck and began to study the Sunday school lesson. I made up my mind that I wouldn't let it get me down. The brother that gave me the car invited me to worship with him. I gave my testimony about that truck asking the pastor to pray for me. We had a glorious time in the Lord I was glad I went. I was invited to preach that evening. The anointing was so high; little did I know this would be the last time, I would preach for over a year. I kept seeing myself doing one-on-one ministry. It was not plain, but I knew I was not in a suit as I was ministering. I kept seeing people crying out but I could not understand. God was trying to tell me something.

I rested and waited for the task at hand. Around 3:00 a.m. I was awakened. I had to read I King Chapter 13 again. I couldn't figure out why I had to keep reading this. I tried to go back to sleep but I couldn't. Before I knew it I had to have my 6:00 a.m. prayer. I started to think about that 3:00 a.m. wake up wondering what that scripture had to do with me. I just didn't understand.

I went to breakfast then went back to the pallet yard. I was greeted at the yard with; "I sure hope you get that truck running today. You have to move it today." What a way to begin a Monday morning. I had the motor in the car ready to come out in an hour. I took the motor in the truck loose, ready to come out in a half hour. I was making progress in a short time. When I finished taking the motors loose the forklift driver came to my aid. Since I was well rested and not frustrated it didn't take long. When I finished I was glad to drive the truck back to the motel.

When I got to the motel I couldn't park at the motel because I had the truck and the trailer. I pulled over to the empty lot where there used to be a restaurant and left the truck there. I went to eat thinking I would wait until Tuesday to go back to Virginia, to bring more pallets back to North Carolina. I began to look at that Scripture in I Kings. It began to minister to me. Even though I really didn't know what God was trying to tell me? I began to really study it.

I wanted to go back to that all I care to consume buffet but the truck wouldn't start. Here we go again. I didn't want to worry about it. I went across the street to eat at the diner. When I finished my meal, I went back to try the truck again when someone saw the hood up and tried to give me a hand. We determined that it should have started because it had fire and it was getting gas. I stopped trying to call my son-in-law to find out what time he was coming to prepare to tow the truck home. He then told me he was glad I called, because he wouldn't be able to come until Wednesday.

I had a day of rest, before it was time to eat turkey with all the people that asked me to fellowship with them for Thanksgiving. This was the first time I was going to eat with people I didn't know like family. Just about anywhere in the south, people open their homes to you. I was invited to fellowship at three different homes in Ahoskie, NC

I told everyone that I was about to go back to Henderson, when my son-in-law came to pick me up. They were all upset, because they had made special provision for me. I asked them to pray to ask that

God's will be done. That opened up a can of worms because they all thought, I would eat with them. I had a real problem, because my daughter wanted me to eat with them also.

I laid down at the motel and rested, and dreamed the weirdest dream. I couldn't remember it, but it was weird. To be honest with you it was more like a nightmare. All I remembered was in the dream it appeared I was homeless. I was really blown away with the thought of me being homeless. I had invested the money I made very well, and I had a good nest egg to retire with and just couldn't see me homeless.

I decided that my dream meant that I would meet someone that looked like me, who I would have to help, that was homeless. Make some kind of provision for him. One thing I had a habit of doing was giving to the homeless, the poor and needy. This was nothing new for me. Everything I was experiencing was what I was used to doing.

Whenever I went to buy a suit if someone went with me, I would buy them one also. Whenever I wore a pair of shoes if someone commented how nice they were, I would ask their size and buy him a pair. Whenever I preached somewhere, if someone told me they liked my tie, if it was not a gift, I would take it off and give it to them.

Whenever I would hear someone's testimony about how they believed God for a car. I would go to the car lot to buy them something dependable and up to date, give them insurance and tags for a year. Don't let me hear someone's appliance went out. I would take their pastor with me, and get them whatever they needed.

I ran into that, Nicholas again. He began to tell me that his wife wasn't going to wait for him because she had met somebody else, and they were going to get married. He didn't have that fire he had when I met him. I could tell he was sorry he had let substances (drugs and alcohol) cause him to behave in an unloving manner.

She was not convinced that he had changed. Furthermore, she wasn't going to let him prove that in time she would see he had changed. Her mind was made up. Nicholas wanted us to pray. He also wanted me to meet her to try to talk her into waiting. I told him if I was available I would talk to her.

I had made commitments to fellowship with other families, but if Nicholas came by, I told him to leave me a message and let me know when he would return. It was early, yet I was tired and wanted to go to sleep. I showered, packed all of my things so that when my son-in-law arrived, I would be ready for him to take the truck, and all of my important papers with him.

I felt like this was the last time I was going to see him in a long time. When he came up with the wrecker to tow me home little did I know that God had a different plan. Finally we separated and I went to my room and He went to his. I began to pray for guidance as to what to do for Thanksgiving. Around 2:00 a.m. The Lord awakened me. I didn't know it was time to go on my journey. The Lord told me to go to the Greyhound bus terminal to catch the bus to New York. I began to argue with the Lord, and even to explain to Him I couldn't think of waking my son-in-law up to hear his mouth. He then told me to walk to the terminal. That did it!!!!

I could not even think of walking 10 miles to the terminal. I began to tell God to come down and sit next to me and tell me that again. You know no man has ever seen Him. I sure felt and heard Him though. I was scared. We discussed this again and again. He still told me to go to the terminal with nothing but the clothes I had on my back. I still could not see why I had to walk. After I stopped arguing with Him, I started to walk to the terminal, when a bus driver in route to the terminal stopped and told me the Lord had told him to take me to New York, and that I had no money. It was so strange, because he identified me as a preacher that had no money.

I got on the bus and Matthew the bus driver began to pray for me. When we got to Virginia I met a young lady that was on her way to Wilmington, DE, for the holiday. Her name was Valerie and she went to college in Norfolk and she knew my daughter. We began to talk about the Lord. Valerie was full of the Holy Ghost and she prayed for me and we had church on the bus. I began to feel good about what I was assigned to do. I asked her not to tell my daughter she had met me and that I was going to New York to begin my homeless journey. At this point I began to feel better about my assignment.

CHAPTER TWO

"And he said unto his disciples. Therefore I say unto you. Take no thought for your life, what ye shall eat; neither for the body, what ye shall put on." Luke 12:22

I began to get sleepy as we were traveling. I began to get comfortable because I had calmness in my spirit. I wanted to read my Bible but I couldn't have it with me. I began to think more about not having clothes than anything else. The weather had been unseasonably warm in North Carolina. The further North we traveled the colder it became. When we were close to the Wilmington, Delaware terminal, the driver told me not to worry because he would tell the relief driver about me, and I would have no trouble. I could not believe it was snowing when we got to New Jersey. This weather had me afraid even more. All I kept hearing was that my needs would be met.

I couldn't see how. I didn't have any money. I didn't have anything. When I got off the bus to go into the terminal, I could smell the scent of people that needed to bathe. The foul odor of stale urine was turning my stomach. I walked around only to hear a small group singing. I followed the sound to where people were passing out lunch bags and dinners. The people were busy talking to the people they were handing out food to.

I kept hearing in my spirit a melody of a song, that Mrs. Whitaker had taught our choir to sing in the

60's. I was in the youth choir at New Bethel Baptist Church, where Rev. Dr. James Marshall Whitaker was the Pastor and his wife Mrs. O.M. Whitaker was the music director. Mrs. Whitaker taught us to sing "Near to the Heart of God ". We use to sing it acapella. It is a beautiful hymn. I remember how the people would respond after we sang it. Most of the people would show some kind of emotion. Some would cry others would shout or make some kind of vocal expression.

After I went back a few years; I heard the group even louder as if I was right there. When I kept following the sound I found the group. Little did I know the Lord had placed them there. They were waiting for me! One of the brothers said, "That's him" when he saw me. He spoke to me with a great big smile on his face, "Praise the Lord Brother. How are you?" I told him I was blessed as usual. He then told me the Lord had shown me to him in a vision and when he greeted me my response would be; "I'm blessed as usual." I'm glad I didn't let my circumstances keep me from responding in my usual manner. Look at God!!! He used my response as a form of identification.

The brother that was talking to me was the Pastor of the group that was there. Pastor Austin then told me he had something for my journey. We are talking about God. You know the one that orders our steps. He then gave me a bag that contained things I would need. Check this out. The contents of this bag were so precise; I was blown away when I saw what was in it. God is so amazing!!! This bag had everything that I needed to get me started on my journey. I mean everything. I kind of got spoiled.

This was a state-of-the-art backpack! It had so many compartments it met all of my needs when I learned how to use it. Let me tell you. This bag had seven tee shirts, seven pairs of underwear (in color, too!). There were three thermal tee shirts, seven pairs of white cotton socks, and three pairs of dress socks. The thermal tee shirts were three different sizes. I didn't understand that, but trust me God knew what He was doing. I'll tell you more about that later. Inside were two pairs of jeans; (they were a little larger than I would have purchased) and a pair of dress pants, a dress shirt, one neck tie and three winter shirts. Two of the shirts were smaller than the flannel quilted. That was all I had for winter. That thermal tee shirt and that flannel quilted shirt was my coat. Praise the Lord!!!

The care packet was so amazing and specific. There were razors, shaving cream, deodorant, toothpaste, toothbrushes, three jars of hair grease, hairbrush, a soap dish and twelve bars of soap. Three washcloths and towels were also included. This really blew my mind increasing my faith even more. You see, I wear dentures. I had to have some way to keep my teeth clean and God knew just what I needed. There was a denture brush, cleaning tablets, and a denture bath. Look at God!!!

After I gave thanks unto the Lord the choir began to sing, "There Is a Fountain Filled with Blood." What they do that for? They sang a couple of verses, I began to sing bass with them, and the Glory of the Lord filled the place. We had church. Suddenly all fear was gone. Praise the Lord! Pastor Austin, introduced me to one of the deacons from the church, he took me to his home to meet his family. After meeting the family, I went to bed, had a very peaceful rest, and was awakened to the smell of bacon frying. God had told them, not to offer me any breakfast because I fast on Fridays. I couldn't help it, but fear began to creep in again. I was all right because; I had rested in a peaceful home among saints. Sleeping in the house with brothers and sisters in Christ is no comparison, to sleeping with total strangers with issues that you totally don't know.

We had prayer and my day began right back at the Port Authority, where pastor and I met back with some of the members from that anointed choir. We sang a few hymns when they asked me to sing one for the road. Someone asked me if I knew "My Soul Is Anchored in the Lord"? That had always been my strength song. As I was singing it something was happening to me that I couldn't explain. I believe God was allowing me to sing this song to become my testimony and power song. Whenever I needed to get closer to Him, I could sing that song. I would sing it or hum it every day.

After a brief moment we began to pray then the

journey began. I walked around with the deacon to see some of the people that were begging and trying to stop people for food and whatever they could get from them. I kept looking at this little old lady. She kept looking like she was up to something. She kept looking at me smiling. I was really tired of looking at people. That little old lady was up to something. She came over to me with a smile that wouldn't quit then said. "Son, I have something for you. The Lord told me to send you where you have to go. Here is your ticket to go where you need to for the next few days. Remember I Kings 13 and I will be praying for you every day." She gave me a great big hug and a kiss then told me she was glad God allowed her to meet a man of such great faith.

I was relieved that I had a ticket to go to New Jersey. Somehow I was able to go to Newark, Trenton, and Camden on that same ticket. I stayed in each city for one to three days that was three days too long. When I got to Newark I met this brother that told me where everything was and how to find help in any city. This brother was more like a drill instructor. Instead of shaving, I was told to always grow a beard, so I could stay alive and fit in. I didn't know how I was going to make it by not shaving.

I then inquired as to when and where we would shower. He laughed so hard then replied, "You would truly be blessed, if you could take a shower." If we were able to get into the shelter, we would have to shower in order to get a bed. I really had a problem now. First I was told I couldn't shave and now I couldn't shower. I didn't want to think about where we were going to sleep.

This brother was a born again believer. I mean he loved the Lord! He knew that I loved the Lord and was on a special assignment. He had been out there for quite a while, so he had the information on everything. He told me where all the free stuff was, where to hang out if it rained, the best place to hang out early in the morning, and where to go to receive money from people without you even asking for it, where you could take a shower twice a week, and all of the soup kitchen spots in town.

I tell you one thing I did a lot of walking. Every day I would walk - excuse me I did a lot of walking and I mean country miles, thank you! I began to thank God for brother Dominick, and at the same time I was trying to get a release. I kept praying asking God how long before I got started. I also kept being reminded of how blessed I was. I truly thanked God for choosing me for this work. Here I have a church without walls.

CHAPTER THREE

"Though I speak with the tongues of men and of angels, and have not charity, I am become as sounding brass, or a tinkling cymbal." 1 Corinthians 13:1

When I arrived in Trenton, New Jersey I was on my own. I was so afraid I didn't want to leave the bus terminal. I stayed there for as long as I could. In order to eat I had to walk to the soup kitchen. I really didn't trust the guy that wanted me to walk with him to the soup kitchen, so I elected to catch the bus hungry to go to Camden, New Jersey.

As I was on my way to Camden, I had to pray and believe that God would protect and comfort me, as fear began to creep in again. After being in the company of brothers and sisters in the Lord, I found myself with nobody to talk aloud with about the Lord. I was always talking to the Lord silently in prayer.

I thought since it was Sunday morning, I would just find a Church close to the bus terminal to attend. I chose this Pentecostal Church, because I felt like I needed to go to a church where they would have testimonies so I could possibly get a song in. I went thinking I would be accepted dressed like I was. Wrong! I didn't have a suit.

You know that statement come as you are because God don't look at the clothes but the heart. I didn't know why it would make a difference but it did. I was sitting up front in the church, and was asked to move in the rear of the church. This was because someone was making a video of the service and because I had no suit on, I would mess up the video! I was so hurt and for the first time in my church going life, I wished I had not gone to this church.

The devotional leaders came up to start the service to read the scripture and to have prayer. The devotional leader started out the testimony service by giving his testimony. I thought he was preaching instead of testifying. When he finally finished, he asked if anyone had a testimony or a song. I stood up but someone in front of me began to sing a song or testify each time. I tried over and over again, but could not say a word or sing a song. It appeared as if they were afraid of me and didn't want me to say a word. I almost lost it. The pastor came out, and they cut off the testimony service.

Because, I was a visitor I thought they would acknowledge me or give me a chance to testify. I didn't know what the Lord was trying to show or tell me. When the service began I felt out of place. I sat through the announcements and choir singing. I enjoyed the choir and the children's moment. There was something about loving strangers told to the children. *"Let brotherly love continue. Be not forgetful to entertain strangers: for thereby some have entertained angels unawares."* *Hebrews 13:1-2* was read, and I was really surprised. I thought what did that have to do with children?

What really struck my heart was the pastor's sermon text that came from 1 Corinthians 13. The topic was "Where Is the Love?" He preached, I mean he preached. The whole time I sat there I asked the question; why can't I say anything? I kept sitting there.

Then there was an offering. Of course I didn't worship in giving because I didn't have one cent. I was invited to go to the table. Because I had no offering I refused to go. I was told to go and touch the table so that the next time I would have an offering to give. I thought that was so strange!

After the offering the pastor acknowledged my presence. I was given a chance to speak. I could not understand why but I couldn't say a word. The whole time I was sitting there, I was thinking of what I was going to say. I really wanted to ask what did Hebrews 13:1-2 have to do with children's church and why was he preaching about love and they showed me no love?

I really had to seek the Lord as to what this was all about. I could not understand why I was speechless when I really had a lot to say. I was being humiliated but couldn't say a word. Because I was told not to tell anyone I was a preacher, I began to cry out to God, "what is this all about?"

I spent another couple of days in Camden and couldn't stand the way things were going. I met a homeless brother at the bus terminal who asked me where I was going to stay for the night. I told him that I didn't know. He took me to the shelter where he was staying. I tried to get a bed, but they told me I had to call this 1-800 number to get approve of my staying. I was glad it was a toll free number. When I called they asked me for the number of the phone I was calling from because they had to call me back. It was cold out there. I waited and waited but no call. I called back but they told me I had to wait for the call back at that number. I told them it was cold and that I was tired of waiting.

I was then told I could go back to the shelter to try to get in. Without an authorization number they could refuse to let me in. I prayed, I went back and I requested to stay and was given that toll free number again. I said I couldn't go through that again. I tried several hours ago. I was then asked from where I called? I told them a pay phone down the street. They laughed and said that was the problem. The pay phones cannot receive incoming calls. The brother asked them to call for me, because he was waiting with me, and no one called back. They did, finally I was permitted to stay for two days. After that I had to see a counselor in order to extend my stay. I was never talked to or given the chance to see the counselor so I have no clue of what that was all about.

If I didn't have a change of environment soon I felt like I was going to lose my mind. God didn't see it that way. He didn't make provisions for me to leave. I went to this soup kitchen and found plenty of love there. They sang hymns on request. I began to see the homeless respond in a very positive manner. Instead of me complaining I was observing more. That is when God moved me, as if I had a test and passed it. I found a ticket to Richmond, VA and on the bus I hopped!

CHAPTER FOUR

"The steps of a good man are ordered by the Lord: and he delighteth in his way." Psalms 37:23

The hardest part of the journey was the thought of me going to Norfolk, Va. I kept hearing the Lord say to prepare to go to Norfolk. He sent me to Ashland to the campground so I could be strengthened for the journey. I went to pray and to lay before the Lord to make sure He was fine tuning me for what I had to do, so that I could get focused. I knew that as long as I was at the campground around the powerful and anointed saints of God, I was going to get words from the Lord that would put me on the straight and the narrow path. In other words, they would let me know without a shadow of a doubt if I had not heard right. As if God didn't already prove Himself over and over again.

I couldn't do anything when I got there but hear word after word about how God had chosen me for a work that many men would not be able to do. You are being taken to a new faith level in the Lord; they kept telling me how God was preparing me for a great work with the poor and needy, that I was going to do a lot of one on one ministry. They knew I was being molded to work with the homeless. God was about to take me to HOMELESS BOOT CAMP.

I guess the greatest fear of going to Norfolk was to have to face people with whom I had grown up. You see I was raised in Portsmouth, Va. This was just a few minutes from Norfolk. The mere fact I use to sing at a lot of Churches in Norfolk, Portsmouth, Chesapeake, Virginia Beach, and Suffolk cause me to be well known in the tidewater area. My mother was always being asked about me. As any mother would do she would tell them about how I was driving tractor and trailer, that I had bought a truck and was doing fine. She would also tell people that I had become a preacher, and that she rarely saw me but, I would call quite often usually every week. I knew that because my status had changed I was not going to be able to call her for a while. Although she would worry about me, I didn't want anyone that knew me to see me and tell her I was in a state of homelessness. God assured me that He would order my steps so that would not happen.

I began to take full advantage of the fact I could now take showers and shave. I was reminded about the need to grow a beard, so I could really fit in. There again I still couldn't shave. Oh, well, it was better that I didn't shave because whenever I would grow a beard my face would itch very badly and break out and I had gotten pass that.

I began to concentrate on why the Lord had sent me to the campground. I ran into people that knew me who began to tell me that I was a man of "Great Faith." I was a chosen vessel for the Lord to teach many of my experience from the assignment the Lord had given me. One person told me I had an angel on my shoulder and that he was assigned to me for the journey. I wanted to ask why he was on my shoulder. I figured they walked right beside us, or that he could do his job from a distance just as long as he watched and protected me.

I was also told to remember the scripture the Lord had me to read and to pay close attention to the voice of God. I was reminded not to ask anyone for anything and to tell no one that I was a preacher. I was also instructed not to try to help God by taking a job for wages, until God released me because that would get me sidetracked and I would be out of the will of God. For some reason I was not liking this stop at all. Of course most of the times when we have something special to do for the Lord we rarely like it. I didn't know how I was going to get all of this faith everybody was talking about. I just kept hearing everything I had need of would be provided for me.

I began to really seek the Lord about what I was doing. I had to know that what I was doing was pleasing Him. I felt that because, He had provided everything for me that I was doing the right thing. I was concerned about what I was experiencing, and the fact I could not rebuke anyone for the way they were treating the homeless. From what I had seen in New Jersey I was glad to be moving to the South. I felt I had to pray without ceasing for the homeless and the people that were serving in the soup kitchens and at the shelters. I rarely ever heard anyone speak in a manner that would draw people to the Lord. I often said if this was an example of Christ, and I was lost I wouldn't want to change either. I was being humbled and drawn to a place of humility as well as an open shame for the way people represented the Lord.

Well, as the hour drew near that the services began at the camp; I was being fed the word. I really missed good old fashioned services where people tapped into the presence of the Lord. It was quite refreshing. I was not in a hurry to get prayed for because, I didn't want to hear any words about the journey on which the Lord had me on. At this place when people prayed for you, it was personal and prophetic. During praise and worship you could get whatever you wanted from the Lord. The praise and worship teams really knew how to take you into the presence of the Lord.

I really looked forward to the early Morning Prayer, the intercessors were really anointed. Sometimes I would go to breakfast real early then go into the woods to be alone with the Lord, come back to the prayer so that my day would really be presented to the Lord for whatever He had for me. I just wanted more and more of Him. I began to seek His face. God began to send more and more people to encourage me. I was glad to be chosen for the homeless journey because God began to show me a lot of wounded people that He was healing.

I began to see the homeless in a different light from what I had been seeing. For some reason I was beginning to see the homeless as Preachers and Teachers. I couldn't wait to get to Norfolk, Va., or wherever else He wanted to send me. I always wanted to do something to help the poor and the homeless so now I had an opportunity to do it firsthand. God allowed me to become just like them. I'm glad my situation was temporary so that one day I would be doing seminars on how to address the needs of the homeless.

I was told that I was going to write a book about my journey and this book was going to be a best seller. I don't mind being honest about someone saying that they saw it becoming a movie also; I could not see it. Well, I began to mingle among the people and it looks like everybody had a word for me. I was tired of hearing about this journey and great faith. I had to get out of here.

Just as I was about to make up my mind that I didn't want to hear anything else about it, I met Jack and Jill. They became a great blessing to me. Jack gave me his personal Bible after he became my friend. Jill told me that she would always be praying for me. Somehow whenever I needed prayer, I would see her in the spirit praying for me. It was a divine connection. I had to get ready for Norfolk. God told me to have someone to take me to the bus terminal.

After I packed and returned the key to my room, while I was in the office someone was on the phone calling from the bus terminal that needed to be picked up. You see at Calvary they provide transportation to and from the bus terminal if they know you are there. The van driver came in to get the name of the person that called when he saw me standing with my bag and asked if I was going to the terminal. I was glad to say yes because I needed a ride. I got in and fear began to creep in again. I was leaving my comfort zone.

While I was in the terminal I thought, "how am I going to get to Norfolk with no ticket?" Jack and Jill came to the terminal and paid for my ticket. I was so amazed for the first time I wasn't worried anymore.

CHAPTER FIVE

"He that dwelleth in the secret place of the most High shall abide under the shadow of the Almighty." Psalms 91:1

I had the hardest time accepting the fact that I was in homeless boot camp, and now I was reporting for duty. I arrived at the bus terminal in Norfolk Va. around 9:00 a.m. All I could see was homeless people all over the place. They were asking people for money including me. I laughed as I told the brother that asked me for money I was homeless. He thought I was joking and acted like he wanted to fight. I looked him right in his eyes and told him, he didn't want to mess with me then he left me alone.

I went to the rest room and there was a sign that read **NO BATHING, NO SHAVING, NO CHANGING OF CLOTHES, AND NO BRUSHING OF TEETH.** I knew there was a problem. When I finished and went back into the lobby, the manager was asking people that didn't have tickets to leave. It was cleared out quickly. I noticed some of the homeless were using lockers so they didn't have to carry their bags around with them all day. They were even sharing lockers like family. I heard one of the ladies; "say thank God for the dollar man." I didn't know who or what she was talking about. I will tell you more about him later. I promise.

I decided to follow the crowd. I watched some people go toward the Library as others were going toward the housing projects. I went to the Library because I needed to read the newspaper to see what was going on with the football games I had missed. While in the Library I observed the homeless looking in the magazines and suddenly the magazines were looking at them. It appeared everyone was asleep. The security guard was telling people they had to wake up or leave.

Sometimes people would go outside to talk and catch fresh air so they could stay awake. When I asked why the people always were sleepy. They said we couldn't sleep too well in the shelters, or when the churches opened their doors we couldn't sleep too well there either. I asked, what they thought was the problem? I was told that often time's people would be under the influence of something that would make them act up. Because, the shelters and the churches had rules to be followed, they would take their drugs and smoke pot before reporting for the night. By the Church members praying sometimes the people would not be able to rest. This would be the request of the prayer warriors.

Every one hung around the Library, to wait for the van from their favorite serving Church to pick them up and take them to Church for lunch. I went with them and was I surprised. The Pastor, Santos, Theodore, and several Ministers on staff were there. The L-O-V-E of God was present also. They had some choir members present that sang songs; some upon request from the guest [homeless] that were present. I was really impressed as to the level of love I felt.

I could easily see why the homeless were eager to go to this Church. They had a full house every week that I attended. The food was good and the Ministry was outstanding. They would have testimony time and preaching every week. The altar call was unbelievable. I would observe the change in the guest week after week. Eventually the ones that were sincere would get jobs and even found housing. They would find time to come back and thank the people that were hosting the feeding, for their prayers, their time, and their love. I think that was God's way of encouraging the host and letting them know their labor was not in vain. Too bad they only feed once a week.

After the meal we were taken back to the Library, and when we saw someone that was blessed by the group's prayers, and they were no longer in a state of homelessness. They would inquire as to what we ate and what the preacher preached about. When we told them, they would encourage us to keep the Faith. I was so blessed week after week at this church. I wasn't able to go there on Sundays because it was too far for me to walk and I had no bus fare.

We went to the mission in the evening for dinner. I was told to eat; that as soon as I finished, I should make my way down to the lottery spot. Get a grip! Not the state lottery. Let me explain, this was the spot where the members of the NEST [Norfolk

Emergency Shelter Team] would meet to give you a number to see if you were chosen to go to the host Church for the night instead of the shelter. If you were not chosen you had to be at the shelter before the curfew or you wouldn't have anywhere to sleep.

Sometimes there would be over a hundred people in line before they passed out numbers. Here is how it worked. You got a number and they had a container where they drew numbers from zero through nine; whatever number you have as your last number was your number. Whenever they call a number you had to turn your number in, in order to board the bus going to the host church until the bus filled to capacity. I think I was blessed whenever I was able to attend the host church, because they would feed us something before we went to bed, when we were awakened we had breakfast.

I couldn't understand why we were awakened around 5:00 a.m. had breakfast, boarded the bus by 6:00 a.m. and were dropped off by 6:30 regardless of the weather condition. When we were dropped off, we would go to the bus terminal to wait for the Library to open.

After a few days I found out that the mission would feed you twice a day for breakfast and dinner. I also found out who the dollar man was and what that was all about. This Lawyer had a routine wherein every morning he would come by to greet everyone that was homeless with a dollar. He was so sharp he knew if he had given you a dollar earlier in his route even if you tried a change of clothes.

I was really beginning to enjoy going to the different churches that were hosting until one of the host church turned out to be the one my uncle belonged to. I had really been excited until they told us that his church was hosting. Someone told me he met him, and he almost told him he met someone that looked like my uncle, but he didn't know my name.

I stayed in the shelter that week. I couldn't wait until my uncle's church stopped hosting! I saw a couple of people I grew up with at the shelter. It's strange the class clown was homeless as were a couple of highly successful people I grew up with also. I found out the successful ones fell prey to drugs. They could not understand what happened to me, because my sister and brother had told them I was a preacher, and that I owned tractor and trailers. I had to ask them not to tell my family they had seen me, because God had me on a special assignment and they would not understand. Little did I know they didn't understand either?

I decided to go to the Sunday service and breakfast at the mission. I heard that when they had altar call, if you went up, you would be able to eat early, otherwise, you would have to wait in a long line to eat where sometimes they would run out of food. I watched people go up for salvation week after week only to eat early. Wow! No WOW!!!

I was told about the circle, which was a place the

members of this church would come out to minister to the homeless every Sunday afternoon. So I went. Guess what? One of my good friends name Lexie was in charge of that ministry. When Lexie saw me she was really surprised. Lexie could not believe I was in a state of homelessness. We went to talk and have coffee. After I explained what I was doing, she was happy for me and she put me on the spot the next week, by asking me to pray at the end of the service. She had me to speak the week after that.

I was invited to her brother's house to stay with them for a couple of weeks. When I met her brother Jason, I was being used by God to help him in a mighty way. I didn't understand at first. I was really happy not to have to deal with the shelters and soup kitchens for a while.

I couldn't take a job or work for money. Jason had a pickup truck that needed repair. We went to the junk yard to get parts and I repaired it in a couple of days. He was so happy about the arrangement, every time the phone rang he was telling everyone he spoke too and they couldn't believe it. You see Jason was touched by the Lord to deal with his sickness with a new faith. He was doing things he had not done for a while.

He had been ill and wasn't getting out much. It was like something in him was awakened and we bonded like brothers. His sister went to work, and I was glad to see her when she returned. We talked about how; Jason was really changing right before our eyes. He got better quickly. He was recovering from what appeared to be a stroke. I never asked what had happened to him.

Jason and I went shopping for some shoes and a coat for me. Because I wear a size fifteen shoe we couldn't find any in my size. He also tried to find me a coat. What a job. We went to the army and navy store and found me a Government Issue rain coat. I was able to stay warm and wear it to church also. What a blessing he was to me. However I felt I was being side tracked and needed to go back to the shelters.

I began to get in trouble because he let me use his pickup, and I decided to go back to Calvary. I drove his truck there, to stay for the whole weekend but failed to call him. I wasn't authorized to do that. I looked up to see that his sister and he were there to pick it up. I was blessed not to have gone to jail. They left without me. He was very angry. I know everything I had done to help him was washed away with my actions.

I told Lexie, I was going for the one night. That's how she knew where I was. She was supposed to go with me. Something happened she didn't go, and she didn't want to tell Jason, but in order to keep him from calling the police, she brought him there rather than to trust me to drive it. I felt I had lost two friends at once. I waited before I went in to the prayer and the first service. Because they left before I could apologize or explain. I knew I had to thank

God it didn't get ugly and to ask Him for forgiveness.

I can't explain why I felt I had to go back to Calvary. I thought by staying at the house rather than at the shelter I had messed up. I knew I was not doing everything to remain with the homeless being in the comfort of that home.

I remember Jack and Jill telling me I had to go back and stay focused. They took me back to the bus terminal and put me on the bus back to Norfolk. He gave me their phone number to call them for prayer. Whenever I was led to call they would always lift my spirits.

CHAPTER SIX

"Trust in the Lord with all thine heart; and lean not unto thine own understanding.In all thy ways acknowledge him, and he shall direct thy paths."Proverbs 3:5-6

I got back in Norfolk early. I was happy to meet Miss C. She worked for Greyhound. You talk about the Lord strategically placing someone on a job that was Miss C. She was a beautiful, compassionate and loving woman, about {middle} age. I talked to her every day that she worked if she was not too busy. I looked forward to seeing her daily.

When she spoke to the homeless, they had a high degree of respect for her, not like the disrespect they would direct toward management. It was as if they knew she was nice, but she didn't take any mess. So they had sense enough not to try her.

We had a very good relationship. When I would talk to her after seeing things not becoming of the Lord, it was like a breath of fresh air. She would always tell me to pray. It was like the Lord would let me vent but not murmur and complain. Miss C made me feel comfortable enough to talk to her about everything.

She knew I was a man of God. I couldn't tell her I was a preacher but she knew. One day out of the clear blue sky she said "the Lord chose the right one for the job you have." I could do nothing but smile. Every morning I would be reading my copy of the

Daily Bread. You know that devotional book! It would always give me strength for the day. When I had a chance to, I would read it aloud for the homeless and pray for them before we went our separate ways.

I found out that in the mornings five days a week there was a Catholic organization that would meet at what the homeless called the wall. You talk about using what you have to really meet the need. They would have devoted and committed volunteers to come up in their personal cars following what looked like a church van. The van would have folding tables and the food. They would set up the tables and the homeless would line up with order.

These volunteers would greet you and really make you feel welcomed. Their smiles were genuine and warm, often times someone would come up to you and say "You look like you could really use a hug" and you would get a warm one. You just wanted to be there when they were serving. They would have a great big pot or two of hot cereal, two sandwiches, something sweet, and a hot beverage with condiments. If you needed something you could request it, if it were available, you would get it in a day or two if they didn't have it in the van. I am talking about clothes that were donated to their ministry.

I was glad I was mingling more, because I was able to learn more about other ministries and helps. There was a place, where this grey haired lady had the appearance of a grandmother type. This sharp dressing young man that was in his late sixty's or early seventy's allowed the homeless to come in and shower, do laundry, grab a bite to eat and even use clippers to cut hair. There really was no excuse for people to have an appearance of homelessness, because of all that was available to them.

If you got a job, and it was verified but you needed transportation to and from work, bus tickets were available. If you needed boots they were provided. If you needed a social security cards, Identification, a physical address, phone calls, or a phone number for job contacts you could use that address and phone number. They even had counselors available to help people cope with their situations. I would always pray for this lady. I thought if she had more money for that ministry she could do more.

I began to ask the question, why?

- Why was it some of the people were homeless and their family members were coming to visit them at the shelter?
- Why was this man married and his wife and kids would come to visit but he couldn't go home with them?
- Why was I hearing from time to time that if I had only done right by my family I wouldn't be out here?
- Why was I hearing that if I had saved money while I was working, I would have something

to fall back on?

Let me try to address some of the whys? Some of the people were abusive to their families, whether verbally, physically, or financially. Most of the time I heard that if it wasn't for the drugs and alcohol I would still have. Plenty of times, people would lie to family members and friends to get money to support their habits and never repay. Often times that made people have tough love in hopes they would turn around.

I even talked to some of the wives and family members. They would tell me they had taken all they could, so they turned it over to Jesus. They figured they would just wash their hands, and see them in a Christian environment being healed. They felt they had to visit to let their loved ones know they cared and still loved them.

I met plenty of people that requested I pray for them for strength. I guess because I was being so nosy, they felt comfortable talking to me. They knew by my response when they spoke I loved the Lord. I had been told I should have been a counselor or preacher or something. Many times I could only laugh and just offer prayer.

I met this brother that had gotten bit by the Aids bug because of sharing needles and having sex with multiple partners. Yet his beautiful wife was praying for him and believing God to give her a saved and healed husband back. I ministered to them and led him to the Lord. He was grateful that I was not afraid of him like most people. Because he looked like walking death, I could understand why people were afraid. I kept watching him change right before my eyes. He was beginning to gain weight and grow his hair back. What a miracle!

I was so in need of finding a place to pray and cry out to the Lord, that the very next morning I went to a few churches in the immediate area and I was turned down over and over. I went to the bus terminal to tell Miss C. She said, "Pray and ask God to lead you where you can go". I told her I had done that. It was too cold to go to the water. I always found that to be a good place. There were no woods around either.

I began to walk toward the park when this brother driving a van reminded me of that fireball Nicholas that I met in Ahoskie, N.C., pulled up and was trying to minister to me. I had to inform him I was already saved. He felt the Lord had directed him to me, because he had to turn around to come back to me.

He told me he thought I was homeless and had a need; he would try to be a blessing to me. I told him I was homeless that I was trying to find a secret closet. He told me he had the keys to the church he attended, that we could go there. I was surprised he knew I had to pray, and that I called it a secret closet. God knew because He sent him right to me. What a blessing! We went to the church, three hours later we were still praying. I was so happy I had a place to call on Jesus in secret.

I remember telling this brother about the calling on his life. He told me he wasn't a preacher. I remember telling him the Lord had chosen him to preach, and when he preached his initial sermon I would be there to witness it. I will tell you more about that later I promise — much later, but I will tell you more.

I found out their order of service and went to church there. I also found out they fed one day a week. I was really glad to meet that brother. God was really meeting all of my needs and the more I asked the more He did.

I meet the Pastor of the brother, Walter Victor. What a blessed man of God and a true servant of the Lord. When I met him we fellowshipped as if I had known him for years.

I liked the love I felt there so much that I would invite other homeless to go to the church with me on Sundays. They enjoyed it so much they wanted to go every time the doors were opened. You know they had to like it because it was a thirty minute walk from the bus terminal where we would meet up to take the walk together.

CHAPTER SEVEN

"A man that hath friends must show himself friendly: and there is a friend that sticketh closer than a brother." Proverbs 18:24

I began to like going to the lottery spot early. You got a chance to talk and mingle. If you were early enough, you could meet some of the host; you know the people from the host Church. I was really surprised to see a husband and wife that were homeless. The women never had to go through the lottery thing. Sometimes the husband would not be chosen so he would make her get off the bus. The women never went through the lottery they just got on the bus. No way would he permit her to go to the church without him.

When you went to the church to sleep the men would be in one area and the women in another. They always had male and female hosts. Even when he went he could not sleep with her. You had to stay dressed when you slept also. Sometimes the guys would be betting his number wouldn't be called. I was told to never throw your number away because if his number wasn't called they would have to call another when she got off.

One night the host church came early enough I saw one of my old teachers, Mr. Williams, he was some teacher. I remember he was fresh out of college when he taught me in high school. I had given him a hard time, and had to ask him to forgive me for the way I had treated him. He had asked about me and learned I was a preacher and that I had my own business. He could not understand what had happened or why I was homeless. I thanked him for investing in me when I was his student. If I remember correctly I was a "B" student in his class. I told him I was on a special assignment from the Lord.

I met one of the brothers from his church and his Pastor. When I first met Brother Jake he and I didn't get along too well. When I got to know him it was on. We got along very well, and as it would turn out he was a very good man. If I were to compare him to any of the disciples it would be Peter. Brother Jake didn't take any mess. He was a praying man that would pray and ask God not to allow anyone to bring alcohol into their church. When a brother tried to board the bus with a forty ounce he dropped and broke it. It sent a message to all of the others not to try it because there was an announcement: God answers prayer, we prayed that no one would bring any alcohol into the church.

I wished I had a church full of Brother Jake's. He had a way with the homeless that were unlike anyone I had met. He could talk to everyone and he had a way of finding out whatever he wanted to know. Jake tried to understand everyone and he tried to find good in everyone. He would play the piano, and have a sing along hymns and Christmas carols.

When the Pastor was available he was always present and a part of the hosting. The youth were even hosting and singing one night.

Every night that I went to the lottery while this church was hosting I was blessed to go. It appeared God made sure I went to this church. I remember singing one night. I had to attend the Sunday morning worship to thank the church and encourage them not to give up on hosting. I thanked them for showing so much love. You could tell it was a lot of work and that it was taking a toll on the workers.

Unless you dealt with or lived with some of the homeless, you would have a hard time understanding what it involves. Let me just tell you a little of what goes on. You see the homeless have an odor that they leave behind. We are talking about people having a need for a shower, the smell of stale cigarettes, old liquor, and marijuana. When they stay in an environment without fresh air for a while you are asking for it. We are talking about the homeless staying in the church for about ten hours a day for seven days. I went to where we were sleeping five days after we stayed and the foul odor was still present.

I was really glad the Pastor let me thank and encourage the members to continue, because regardless to what they had done to clean the odor was still present. That alone would have been enough to make the average group of believers say no-no-no! No more. That's what I call love and commitment. We find the scripture says in 1Peter 4:8-10 *"And above all things have fervent charity among yourselves: for charity shall cover the multitude of sins. Use hospitality one to another without grudging. As every man hath received the gift, even so minister the same one to another, as good stewards of the manifold grace of God."* *I really know why "LOVE COVERS THE MULTITUDE OF SIN".* I know sin stinks but whew!!!

Now you talk about love! These people gave up their Christmas to spend time and show love by giving gifts to the guests. They really made us feel right at home and like family. They gave us cosmetics, T-shirts, gloves, hats and scarves. I hated to see the day we would not be coming back to this church. All good things must come to an end.

Well, because of the holiday we had a church hosting that was in walking distance, no lottery, you just reported to the church. You talk about the difference between night and day. You would think the Pastor would want to be more involved in greeting the guests. Not this pastor. I made it a point to meet him.

After about three days of them hosting. They had a funeral and I made it a priority to be there. I got an appointment with him. I told him the homeless wanted him to come as had the other Pastors at other churches. He told me he wanted no parts of the homeless. I asked him why? He told me he would have nothing to do with us bums. I told him he needed to raise his hands, and tell the Lord thank you. He asked why? I told him for one I have no tape recorder, for two that I was saved, sanctified and filled with the Holy Ghosts. He asked what that had to do with anything. I told him if I wasn't saved, I would not have behaved as a saint. Not after that statement!

I asked this man how he became a Pastor. I could not see how a man like him could lead a flock. When the members that hosted saw me, they wanted to know how the meeting went. I told them I didn't want to discuss it. They told me he was about to be ousted as their Pastor. I told them I would be praying for them and left it at that.

I went to the shelter to see the chaplain who asked me if I was a veteran, because the veteran representative was there to see veterans to let us know what was available to us in the way of help. I spoke to the representative. When he verified my status, he gave me a sleeping bag and told me they would be back to pick us up the next morning, to take us to Newport News, to allow us to file for help to possibly get housing and other services. I was glad to get that government issued sleeping bag, because I didn't have to use the mats and blankets they give you at the churches anymore.

After talking to the representative, I was saddened to know the new Chaplain had gotten some news about his mother. That gave me a chance to minister to him rather than him ministering to me. When we met I was blessed to give him a nugget or two about my gift. I encouraged him to be strong. I knew in a few days he was going to have to make the trip back home to bury his mother. I also told him he had to be strong for his family. We had prayer, and I shared a Scripture with him. He thanked me, and told me that when I finished my journey I should go back to being a Pastor.

I had accumulated a lot of stuff and had a need for one of those lockers. You know when there is a need God always makes the provision. Check this out. I remembered the dollar man and I figured if I caught him every morning I would be able to pay for the locker. Wrong! He didn't make that trip on Saturday, or Sunday. I was given a locker number by God to use and I took it. Low and behold when I went to it, I was told to pull it open, to put my gear in it, to close the door and remove the key. I did and guess what; I needed no money for as long as I needed that locker. If you didn't put a dollar in it every day you would lose your gear.

I went back to the mission and was told to see the head chaplain to take on the security job for the programmers. I agreed to do so and was granted the second shift. My job was to make sure the feeding went orderly that no one went up to the sleeping quarters without authorization. I didn't like the job so I quit within a week. Every time I saw a need to minister to one of the homeless I was told I couldn't. Houston we had a problem. I had to stop because I was finding out more than I needed to know about the mission.

I met this group of Seventh Day Adventist that were serving who invited me to spend the Sabbath with them at their church. I asked for the address and when they told me where it was I knew I wasn't about to walk. No ride, no church and I wasn't ashamed to tell them either. I was ready to be picked up early Saturday morning to go to church. It was strange for me going to church on Saturday and Sunday but I enjoyed it. Everyone was told I was one of the people from the shelter where they fed.

When they knew that they treated me like a king. There really wasn't much love shown, but it was like they were glad the people that worked on that committee recruited people to come to their church. I guess because they had prepared food from their private homes and brought it to share. I was invited to have dinner with them and we had a little fellowship. They had another service after eating to close out the Sabbath.

If I had to evaluate these people as a homeless person to see if I would attend again I would not have done so. I went back for both services every week that I remained in Norfolk. There was a brother there that talked to me as if we had known each other for years. Because of this brother I visited his home and continued to fellowship with them until it was time to move on to Florida. On Sundays I went back to going to the Church where I was able to pray with Dominick, the brother that had the calling on his life.

They treated me like family there and I enjoyed every service I attended there.

CHAPTER EIGHT

"Now unto him that is able to do exceeding abundantly above all that we ask or think, according to the power that worketh in us." Ephesians 3:20

I was relieved I had met so many warm people that really gave me encouragement and hope to continue being obedient to the Lord and hang in there. Early Monday mornings I always looked forward to seeing the dollar man, and to go to that church with so much love. Around 11 or so the van would make its rounds. I was always at the library to check out the scores of the football games and read the Bible.

I really couldn't understand why they would take us back from the host church, or make us leave the church so early regardless of the weather. I guess we were to be grateful we had somewhere to stay from the elements at night. I talked to the man that was in charge of the NEST (Norfolk Emergency Shelter Team) program and asked why that was. I can honestly say I got no satisfactory answers. That stayed in my heart all day. I tried to understand what I was supposed to learn from this.

The way I figured it, all I could do was to keep praying. I went over to the place where that sharp dressing old man and that grandmother figure worked. I had a chance to talk to her and she enlightened me about the problems with trying to do more. She desired to have a bigger budget so she could do more, but she didn't. She desired to have a bigger facility and a larger staff, but she didn't. She desired to have more donations to come in and while we were talking she did; food that is. We had to terminate our conversation so she could get the donations put up.

Of course I helped, volunteering to help in whatever capacity I could. I was then asked if I would clean the rest room, "of course" I replied, and cleaned them. I then waited until all of the guests would leave to mop. I was asked why I worked so hard to help. I said, "I wanted to be an example to the guest so that they could learn that when we make a mess we should clean it up". I think that was my way of showing her she had help; she just had to ask for it.

After a great day I saw the man from the NEST program and I was surprised. I mean I was surprised! He looked like he had been in a battle. I found out one of the homeless had beat him down. I couldn't find out what happened. I just heard him say he had to forgive him and go on because he wasn't going to let this incident stop him. He looked like he should have been admitted to the Hospital. I inquired as to what happened, who had done this to him? He would not reveal this information to me.

We had the lottery and for the first time in a long time my number was not chosen. I had to go to the shelter. I really didn't want to go there after going to the churches. I liked to meet different host to see how they met the needs of the homeless. I felt something was about to change again. I was feeling the need for a change. Too much was happening that I couldn't understand nor explain and it was too fast.

I was getting feed up with what I was seeing and couldn't do anything about it but pray. My prayer was mainly asking God to have mercy. You know that short prayer we have a tendency to pray when we really don't know what else to say or do. When we know we are not doing what we are supposed to do to represent God in the fullness.

I couldn't wait to go to the circle to see my friend. Lexie introduced me to some of the members of her church. I really remember the twins I met, Bridget, and Brook. I was refreshed every time when I was in their presence. What precious women of God. They showed so much love to everyone they met. I really knew why everybody had to go to the circle every Sunday afternoon. When the time came for them to close you wanted to go to the evening service with them. If you went, you would have to sacrifice the lottery and had to go to the shelter but I didn't care. I had to go to the church.

They had a praise and worship team that really knew how to usher in the presence of God. You could really feel Him in the room. I got what I needed during the praise and worship. When it was time for the Word I was ready for it. I enjoyed it so well I wanted to tell the Pastor and to shake her hand. I was not permitted to do that. Security would not allow me to. I went to high school and played tennis with one of the security. I asked him if I could see her for a minute but he told me I had to make an appointment. Well, so much for who you know.

I went to the shelter to sleep but after tossing and turning all night, I had to ask the Lord what this was all about. I didn't get any answers. I was glad to go to the Library to see the scores. Before I knew it the scores were watching me. I was told that I had to stay awake or leave. I was so tired I couldn't stay awake and was asked to leave. I had to wait outside in the cold for the van to go to that favorite church.

As I was waiting for the van there were people talking about how the so called Christians were behaving in the different places they were going that fed and that housed us for the night. I was hurt when they were talking about the lack of love in just about everywhere but the church we were waiting to go to. Out of the blue somebody said; that church made up for all the other places we went and they wished they housed us also. The negative remarks made me feel bad and embarrassed for the people they were talking about.

I told them they had to stop watching the people and to focus on Jesus. They would tell me that the only Jesus they were supposed to see was in Christians, but they had a hard time finding Him there. I was speechless because they were telling the truth, and I didn't know what to tell them. I began to pray for the people that were hosting and feeding the homeless more.

When I got to the church, I was glad because the speaker began to speak about seeking the Lord not allowing the negative examples to influence us. He said that when he first came to the Lord, he began to see things differently than when he didn't know the Lord. He also said the faults he use to see in people were different. God had to really change people, and the people really had to want that change. One thing he was certain of was that God loved everyone in spite of the way they represented Him.

I was then told to prepare myself to go to the next place. I had to pack and reduce my load because I was leaving town on Thursday to go to the next state. I was not concerned as to how I was going to go or where I was going. I was glad I was able to go to prayer service before I was to depart. I was hanging around the bus terminal more and more as if my ticket was going to be found laying around on the floor or something.

I was talking to Miss C. when I saw the bus driver that picked me up in North Carolina. I was really surprised when he saw and identified me. He gave me a great big hug then told me he was glad to see me then told me that the weight gain did me good. I could not see how he could remember me with the beard and having added about fifty pounds to my statue. He said it was my voice that gave me away. He told Miss C. that I was a very special man that had influenced his relationship with the Lord to be taken to a new level. She told me that it was rare for him to be at this terminal since he began to run that different route.

Miss C. also told me he was a very special man that had been with Greyhound for many years. Knowing I was about to leave in a couple of days I had to see him so I could be at ease and remember that God was still in charge of what was next. I wasn't worried as to how I was leaving or of the provision. While I was talking to Miss C. my friend told me the Lord told him to pay for a ticket for me to go to Jacksonville Florida and to leave on Thursday. She took a page out of my book and said; "Look at God!!!" He paid for my ticket then we made sure I would be arriving in the morning in Florida, so I could be able to find my way around to the shelters.

CHAPTER NINE

"The Lord is my light and my salvation; whom shall I fear? the Lord is the strength of my life; of whom shall I be afraid?" Psalms 27:1

I arrived in Jacksonville, Fl. I was surprised that they had so many police at the bus terminal. I could see they had a problem with the homeless as they did in Norfolk, Va. I could not but help notice the homeless asked everyone they saw for money. The police presence would keep this down to a minimum. I was asked for money, when I told the man that I had no money for him and he was insulted. I walked away, while he acted as if he wanted to fight.

I was met by a brother that was homeless, he asked me for directions to the shelter. I was surprised because he could see I had an appearance of homelessness. I told him I just came to this city and had no knowledge. He then told me he was staying at the city rescue mission and that he would help me. I was glad because I had a few bags. I thought I was going to get a locker, but they didn't have the same set-up as in Norfolk, Va. They had lockers; however there was a shorter time limit on the use.

We went to the shelter which was about seven blocks from the terminal. I checked in and was quite surprised at the crowd, and the procedure for checking in. I was glad to see so much order plus the respect the people that were in charge had for the guests. I later learned the facility was run by programmers that were also homeless. The security and the greeters met me with much love and compassion. When we went to dinner, I found myself sitting at the table with the man that wanted to fight at the bus terminal. When he realized I was the same person he wanted to fight he was apologetic. He told me his name was Hunter, and he tried to be my friend.

I met this group of brethren from the church which was down the street that were offering to pick up people for their Friday night service. I found out the time and made myself available to go. I heard many people say they were going, but between the time they were invited and the church bus was to pick them up, the devil blocked their going. I could but only observe; again I was in the silent mode.

I was glad to be in service at the church. I was right at home because the church was Pentecostal and they had testimony service, and was I glad to sing my favorite song "My Soul Is Anchored in the Lord". The choir sang, I mean they sang! The Bishop preached, and we had a glorious time in the Lord. I was ready for this town, because I felt this was the church God had placed me in to have a covering. I was invited to join the brothers on Saturday after their radio broadcast and we had a wonderful fellowship.

When I got back to the shelter, I found a basketball

game out back of the shelter. I was challenged to play a couple of rounds. But because of the weight gain, I thought I would not play but for some reason I was told to play, and that would help me to shake some of the weight off. I would have to play every day for hours to cause that to happen. We played a game or two. For some reason I was seeing myself using the basketball as a tool to recruit people to join the army of the Lord.

I had a flash back to when I was in junior high school, when the teachers would play the school team and we would always loose. I also remembered the leaders in the church would play the youth. The leaders would win, and then we had to go to Sunday school and bible study, because we had challenged them and lost. I tell you one thing; by always losing I learned a lot going to the extra services during the week.

I began to play and daily I was being constantly challenged by older people and the youth. It appeared I was always on the winning side except for this one brother that was a victim of the Oklahoma bombing. For some reason I couldn't beat him. Whenever there was a challenge, the person or persons I played had to agree to come to my personal bible study, or to go to church with me when the van came to pick us up. I had people lining up for a game. The study group was getting larger daily.

Well, I guess I had been there about eight days, when I met Elder Hurled who was a Seventh Day

Adventist Minister and the brother could sing too. When people saw us they thought we were blood brothers. He had come to see some of the people that were attending their services on Saturday, and I was invited to come. Of course as with the Norfolk experience I accepted and it was a great service. After the service we ate. Everyone had brought cover dishes and we had a great fellowship. I was being spoiled. I waited to attend the evening service to end the Sabbath.

Later on in the week they had held my bags for me at the shelter and then they informed me they could not hold them any longer. I began to give away clothes that no longer fit me to lighten my load. You would have thought I was the issue room for the shelter. I had no idea I had accumulated so much stuff. I saw Elder Hurled who invited me to come to choir rehearsal. I went and he invited me to sing a solo the next Sabbath and to sing with the choir.

I told him of the problem I had at the shelter with all of my gear then he told me to check on a storage unit at the U-Haul building. To my surprise he took me and paid for a unit. What a blessing!!! I had access whenever I needed to get to my gear, and I was free to travel light.

I had a need for glasses and he took me to another shelter that had a medical facility. I registered and was examined and fitted for glasses. I got them two weeks after the examination. I tried to get my teeth fixed and to get a partial but there was nothing happening. I had to wait about six months. Hello!!! I needed them, like, now!!! However, I was grateful there was a facility to meet the medical needs of the homeless, never-mind the wait or the inaccuracies of the prescriptions.

For some reason I had to take my glasses back because the prescription was not correct in one eye. I was told I had to wait until the doctors came back to be re-tested in order to have them corrected. I had no idea I had to wait another month. I was still without glasses.

It was getting close to Easter, but I had no suit to wear for church that fit me. Hurled and I went to the thrift stores to try to find me something to wear for Church. I was trying to tell him that in my past experiences I was not going to find anything in my size because when people my size got rid of clothes, they would be ready for the garbage. Big people really don't get rid of clothes because they are harder to get.

I thought about how I used to shop and whoever was with me would be treated to an outfit also. I thought because I had invested in giving in the past, that I was about to reap the reward of sowing. Wrong!!! We went to the thrift shop that belonged to the mission, and there was a picture of Jesus that showed him laughing. When Elder Hurled saw it he said "that's what he was talking about that God had a sense of humor." I had to find the owner of that picture, and I talked to him for about an hour, then we had church. However, we couldn't find anything for me to wear.

Finally, I had to go because it was time to meet with the brothers at the church for the Friday night service. I had to eat and prepare to go. I invited several people to go but they all refused. You have to remember they were glad it was Friday also they had previous commitments. I encouraged them that if they wanted to change, and grow in their walk with the Lord, they had to change their environment and friends.

For the first time since I had been going to church with Elder Hurled on Saturday's I had to tell him I was not available this Saturday, because I was going somewhere else. I talked to the minister from the church I attended on Friday night. He and another man of God from the church came to the shelter to preach and they invited me to their Saturday broadcast. I heard them on the radio then went to join them for their street outreach. They had some clothes that were donated so he offered me some sport jackets to try on. To my surprise they used to belong to the Bishop. They fit except for the sleeves but I was not concerned about that. I just knew the Lord would supply someone to alter them for me.

I had two sport jackets I could wear. I was grateful and thought about taking all of the jackets that were available. I was told to leave some for somebody else. My thought was I was not going to find anything else to fit me, but if they were for me they would still be available later. I was so happy I had two jackets. I was hoping I would find shirts and ties that would match. When we returned to the church, I was given the rest of the jackets and shirts and ties. Look at God!!!

CHAPTER TEN

"Let them shout for joy, and be glad, that favor my righteous cause: yea, let them say continually, Let the Lord be magnified, which hath pleasure in the prosperity of his servant." Psalms 35:27

I wanted to share with people I really trusted, who I was and about the assignment. When I was about to share with Elder Hurled, I heard a voice that sounded like that little old lady from New York that gave me that great big hug and ticket saying remember I Kings 13. Then she said he was going to think I was crazy and lying. Then I remembered tell no one you are a minister.

Elder Hurled, and I spent a lot of time together, but he was not clear on whom I was or why we met. I was about to be reunited with judgment in the highest degree. I was introduced to a few people he knew that the Lord allowed me to minister to. I guess because of the prophetic anointing in my life, God chose me for this assignment and allowed me to flow in the gift. I ministered to one of his friends then she shared with him what was said. When he saw me he went off. I didn't know what was said or why he was so upset. I had to pray and seek the Lord as to why I was in this position.

I went to the church on Saturday and saw a brother from the Norfolk church, Justin Lane, that had came to visit his father. He told me that if I had told him I was coming to Jacksonville; he would have given me his father's phone number. I was surprised; God had let us talk about my journey. He was wondering why he hadn't seen me at the Norfolk church anymore. They were stationed in Norfolk, but he grew up in Jacksonville.

I was given Justin's address and telephone number and he told me to call him from time to time. Look at God!!! I had a prayer partner. He was telling me what some people in Norfolk were saying after I left. Thank God Elder Hurled, was listening to the praise reports. He began to tell me about the words people had gotten and how they had come to pass. There was this one family I was close to, and at the time the sister wanted to give up on her husband and I encouraged her to hang in there. Turn him over to the Lord. Now he had turned around for the better. He had told the church he thanked the Lord he met me and he allowed me to minister to him one on one.

I thank God he allowed Elder Hurled to hear, because I thought he and I made a good team. However, there was trouble brewing to cause us to go our separate ways. Thank God he allowed him to hear the praise report of what happened in Norfolk. I was not available to hang with Elder Hurled as much as we used to. God was allowing me to do more one on one ministering with the homeless, and to worship more at other churches.

I was glad to know some of the homeless were going to be baptized at the church right across the street from the shelter. I was glad and sad at the same time. I was glad they were saved and were being baptized. I was sad because I felt by being in a large church they would not get all they needed to grow spiritually, only become lost in the crowd. I was encouraged to go with them to a service or two.

To my surprise we went together, but were treated like outcast. We went early as there were plenty of empty seats downstairs, but we were ushered to the balcony. When I asked if we could sit downstairs, we were told we had to sit in the balcony. I asked why? I was told to be thankful we were able to sit in the balcony. I had to ask the Lord to humble me, and help me to keep peace. I really had to ask Him what I heard Joyce Meyers say many times "Lord Help Me to Keep My Big Mouth Shut." I was blown away.

I found out one of my favorite groups were going to be at a church and I began to pray and ask the Lord to make a way for me to go to the concert. They were charging for the concert and the dinner afterwards. I called the Pastor to ask if there were any complimentary tickets available, because I was in a state of homelessness that I was staying at the shelter, I really wanted to go to the "Witness" concert. I was asked how I found out about it.

When people came to minister at the shelter they would tell us about different things going on at their churches. A brother from the church that was hosting told us about "Witness". Because we sing hymns, he recognized that I knew them. He thought I had a good voice and would really like "Witness". I asked if there were any tickets available for the homeless, if they would have transportation to and from the church for us. I was given the phone number and told to call because it wouldn't hurt to ask.

When I called it was as if no one knew what I was talking about. I was referred to about five different people but no one could tell me anything. I was not accustomed to paying to go to a church concert, but I could understand paying to eat at a benefit dinner. I wasn't hungry for food but my appetite for ministry in music was very high. I just got on my knees and prayed, I asked the Lord to make a way for me to go. After I prayed I got dressed because I just knew God was going to work it out. I went out to the yard in less than 10 minutes after sitting there someone came to see if I wanted to go. Look out that was fast!!!

God was quick. When I stayed still, I made up my mind I was not going to try to help God, or be embarrassed anymore by asking the pastor or anyone else for information about the availability of tickets, God worked it out. I could not imagine what would have happened to my faith, if I had not gone.

I was invited to go to the dinner, someone had purchased tickets for the dinner but their guest couldn't attend, so I was blessed to go. The concert and dinner was good. I thought I was at the finest restaurant, because the food was so delightful. The fellowship wasn't bad either. I told everybody I could at the shelter about the concert and dinner.

People that were supposed to go were sorry they missed it.

I was asked to go to the director's office of the shelter for a meeting. He wanted to know how long I had been staying overnight. I told him I didn't know. He checked the computer, and it indicated I had been there for only one night. He told me that couldn't be accurate because he had seen me there for about ten days. I was then asked why I was there and I replied because I was homeless and needed food and shelter. I was told that I didn't belong there.

I was then informed; if I wanted to stay longer, I had to be enrolled in the program. I asked what program? I was told for alcohol or drug abuse. I said I didn't qualify for either one of those programs. I was asked if I could volunteer for the maintenance department and help around there. I then said "I sure can". I was added to the staff, assigned a different bed and quarters to stay, plus given different times to eat. No more twice a day, now three times a day. I felt special!!!

The need came for more rooms for the women and children, so we made plans to turn this building into more rooms for them. I told the director, I had experience in construction so we got right to it. Before we knew it we were finished, and the women and children were moving in. I was not free to come and go as I was before I was a volunteer. I had a certain number of hours to do every weekday. I really liked it, because I didn't have to walk as much to go to other places to eat lunch.

Every morning we would have open discussions of the Bible. Some mornings the discussion would be so hot you wouldn't want to end them. Of course, we did have to work and had places to go. It was good to have early morning discussions for it would give us strength to handle the darts of the enemy for the day.

When the challengers heard I had a job, and was working all day they thought they would challenge me to some games of one on one basketball. The games would last a little longer, but the result would be the same. I still had the study group when I was finished playing for the day.

There was a big day at the Claire White Mission. I heard the Jaguars were going to be serving the homeless. Since I hadn't gone to any games I wanted to go to the event. It was crowded but they had plenty of food. It was also a fun filled day. The homeless talked about it for a long time. They were impressed that the Jaguars would take time to come and serve us.

I was surprised I was able to go to this park and boardwalk and see the sunset. I think they called this place Riverside. Every time there was a thunderstorm I noticed the clouds more and more. It was like the Lord was speaking to me through the clouds. I was looking in the clouds when I told a friend the Lord was upset, that He was about to uproot some trees. As I walked around I would see evidence of the activities of sin; the Lord was definitely not pleased with what was going on in this park. You would find a lot of kids at the park having a ball chasing each other and playing all kind of games.

I think about three days after I told others about what I saw, it happened. I went to the park with this lady I met and her family. Her car broke down but I was able to help her so she invited me to go with them. I told her I didn't have much time because I had a curfew at the shelter. She could not believe I was homeless. We went to the park and I couldn't believe my eyes, trees were up rooted all over the place in the park.

After spending about an hour at the park, I asked her to take me back to the shelter. She told me I could stay with them. I said I had to go back to the shelter. When we pulled up I saw Harold the security guard. He told me I better hurry because he thought I was late. Thank God I made it.

After I checked in I told Harold what I saw at the park, but I couldn't tell him how to get there to see it. Because he was from Jacksonville, and news travels fast he knew about it already. He asked me how I knew it before it happened. I tried to find out what he was talking about and why he went there. While we were talking the brother I told about the vision I had came up, asked me if I was psychic. I was insulted and surprised he told Harold and a lot of other people. I told him it was going to happen three days before it actually did.

CHAPTER ELEVEN

"Having a form of godliness, but denying the power thereof: from such turn away." 2 Timothy 3:5

I was beginning to enjoy the city of Jacksonville. I really had to stay focused, because I was losing sight on the purpose of the journey. I was seeking evidence for the love of Jesus. Again I was reflecting on Camden, New Jersey the sermon I had heard about love. I felt like I was about to allow judging not discernment take over. I felt I was in a religious town. I guess one could say it was like Paul being in Corinth.

Since I came to Jacksonville I thought I was attending the University of Homelessness. I was enrolled in Homeless 101. I was so amazed there were so many churches that were invited to minister to the needs of the homeless at the shelters. The homeless were not totally changing and were not being delivered. Church people were satisfied with the altar call. Not knowing that the same homeless would have a tendency of responding to altar calls night after night.

I was getting fed up with what I was seeing night after night. I went to a few people and told them to ask questions about what they were doing. I wanted to make sure they understood what they were committing to; when they allowed people to pray with them.

We were told by one of the persons ministering that if we were in the will of God we wouldn't be homeless. If we were Christians we would not be homeless. If we were not alcoholics and drug addicts we would not be homeless.

I raised my hand and told him none of what he said applied to me, and I felt offended by his generalizations. People looked at me as if to say "no he didn't." Yet they agreed with me and some replied "me either"!

After the service I went to the person that ministered, and said to him be sure God was speaking through him when he ministered. I also asked how one can get out of homelessness. I had thoughts of the many people I was in contact with daily that were homeless for different reasons. Here are a few.

- *The women and children that were trusting the husband, and father, to continue to provide for them yet they abandoned them for whatever reason.*
- *Those policemen and fire fighters that were living from paycheck to paycheck but were laid off.*
- *Those people that were committed to that company for twenty years that went bankrupt and because of their age found it difficult to find gainful employment elsewhere after exhausting all of their unemployment benefits.*
- *Those people that were victim of natural disasters; hurricanes, tornadoes, floods, fires etc...*

- *That pastor or deacon that fell and there was no one there to pick them up and help them to be restored.*

I was saddened he had no answers. When we are given an opportunity to present Jesus to someone we think is lost we sometimes miss it, because we try to figure out why? I told him that is not a solution and I just wanted to know some solutions.

I reflected back to how over the years my grandmother would look forward to Billy Graham and his crusades on T.V. When she would make us watch him I would be glad to hear that song at the end you know "Just as I Am". Grandma would be fascinated over how many people would come down for the altar call. She would also say the messages were powerful and Billy Graham never changed.

Since I can remember, I have always said the message of Jesus Christ is always the same, but the method has to change especially when it comes to the homeless. We cannot take for granted a person will come to the shelter or soup kitchen saved, sanctified and filled with the Holy Spirit. We should always take an opportunity to present Jesus to the lost at all cost. To present them to Jesus just as they are, He does the changing, but we have to let Him have His way.

I saw Elder Hurley, he was furious with me about something that was said to his friend. I guess that was the final straw. I had ministered to his friend that worked at another shelter. She apparently didn't understand all that was said but she shared with him and he was furious. I then told him that`s why it was important when I ministered to her he should have been present as a witness. Since the waters were so troubled the time had come for me to leave.

I was told to get Elder Hurley to take me to the bus terminal so that I could go to the ticket counter and get my ticket. I told the lady my name; she told me there was nothing for me in the computer. I just knew I heard the voice of the Lord. I asked her to check again. There was nothing for W. L. Bryant. While I was at the counter a lady that had heard me preach called me "Bishop Bryant"; that was perfect timing. The clerk asked her what she called me. She responded that I was Bishop W. L. Bryant. There was a ticket for me to Norfolk Va. leaving in about an hour. Look at God!!!

I had no identification, I was able to pick up the ticket and go to Norfolk. When I arrived I saw Miss C. She told me that the brother I used to minister with at the terminal, was in the paper to preach his initial sermon today.

CHAPTER TWELVE

"And whatsoever ye do in word or deed, do all in the name of the Lord Jesus, giving thanks to God the Father by him."
Colossians 3:17

I walked to the church as if I was going to a fire. When I arrived I heard Michael Miles saying how he was told by a homeless brother that he would preach but he just couldn't believe it. He also remembered the brother said, he would bear witness of the service, but he didn't see him. I walked in the church right after that statement! It was great, the Lord allowed me to see and hear a powerful man of God. I was glad to be there. For some reason, I felt like it was the end of my journey. I got a chance to see what was said to the man of God come to pass. I was also happy to be back in Norfolk around his Pastor and his Pastor's wife.

That young man preached. He appeared to be nervous, as would be expected from someone that never preached before a crowd of people. I've heard him preach to people one on one. I began to pray for him the nervousness left and he kicked it into high gear. His initial sermon was so powerful. I was excited for him. His message stayed fresh in my mind for weeks.

I was blown away! A couple of days later, I saw his Pastor and wife at this seafood restaurant while I was talking to this brother that had aids. We talked for a few minutes about him then we prayed for him. We just knew the Lord had heard, and answered our prayer to heal him. We left the restaurant; I walked to the shelter to eat. He parked on the same street that the shelter was on. When we arrived at his car there was a parking ticket on it. To my surprise he said the ticket was well worth it because of the prayer.

I talked to the brother we prayed for, his name was Raphael and he told me that when we prayed for him warmth came over him, and he just knew he was touched by the Lord. He also said before we prayed for him he was so weak he felt like giving up on life. He confessed, and was sorry he had contacted the aids virus. He was glad the Lord led him to pass by the restaurant. He said he felt different and he thought he was healed.

The brother told me he wanted to go to the doctors and tell them to run another test, but he didn't know how to explain to them that he thought he was healed. I asked him what was up with that thought he was healed stuff. Then he said he knew he was healed. All I could tell him was to pray and God would do the rest. As often as he could he should thank God, praise Him, and give testimony of what God had done.

The brothers wife Mara, came to visit him at the mission, he told her he got prayer and he knew the Lord had healed him because he felt the healing process when the Pastor prayed for him. As with most of us we discourage people with the fruit of our lips. Her response blew him away; she said no one has ever been healed from aids. He said this was a divine healing from God he felt it and he knew it was so.

I began to think he felt he was alone. The one person he thought he had in his corner tried to kill his spirit. She then said the proof would be if he had another examination from the doctor. He spoke like a man of great faith and said he thought she would have encouraged him to go to church with her and give his testimony. He felt he didn't need another examination, because that would show a little doubt on his part. He was looking for her to be excited with him. She wasn't, so he felt like he was all alone.

I encouraged him to go to the church of the pastor that prayed for him. He responded as far as he was concerned he was through fooling with church folk. I tried to tell him to stop looking at people and to look at the one that created people. He then told me he was so hurt and needed a hug from his wife. He asked her for one but instead of her hugging him she just blew him off. I offered him a hug and he cried like a baby. He told me he felt that the hug was genuine and he felt the power of God just like he did when the Pastor prayed and the Lord healed him.

He asked me where the church of the Pastor was. I told him they had a service starting in about half an hour and we could walk to the church in twenty minutes, he agreed to go. We were walking to the church when he saw his wife again she invited him to go to prayer service with her. To my surprise he accepted.

When I got too the service the Pastor asked me if I had seen the young man we prayed for. I told him I thought I had a surprise for him because I invited him. But on the way walking to the church, his wife saw him and invited him to go with her to prayer service, he went with her instead. I could not see how he could go with her after she doubted his healing and refused to give him a hug earlier. I was really surprised.

The Pastor felt compelled to tell me, as I would invite people to church I should immediately pray that the will of God would be done and there would be no stumbling blocks in the way. Because he could see that I had a love for God and His creation. God was allowing me to be a light to draw the homeless closer to Him, I was delighted to hear those instructions and word from the Lord through him. That was wisdom from an anointed and humble man of God.

For some reason I felt my stay would be very brief. I felt my journey was about to end. I had no idea what was next. I went to pray on the water and it was revealed to me, I was on some kind of welfare. I really didn't understand that. I thought I was finished with the journey. I kept seeing myself in New Jersey in a town called Vineland. I sought the Lord and he made a provision for me to go.

CHAPTER THIRTEEN

"But they that wait upon the Lord shall renew their strength; they shall mount up with wings as eagles; they shall run, and not be weary; and they shall walk, and not faint. Isaiah 40:31

I did not have any idea I had to go back up North. I caught a private bus from Virginia Beach, Va. that went to Atlantic City to the casinos. The bus went to Delaware and crossed the water on the ferry. When we arrived in Jersey we got on a casino express bus and I was given the fare for the bus in a cash voucher at the casino. I ended up in Pleasantville, New Jersey right outside of Atlantic City, New Jersey; this is where I got my ministry foundation under Bishop Carter.

I found myself in a situation saints could only dream of. I was around my mentor and living with him and his family. He had a rule in his house that taught me the power and importance of prayer. We prayed as a family four times a day. The Lord really blessed me with the tools I needed for the importance of praying for others.

In the Carter home you never heard negativity. This man of God really spent quality time with the Lord. He told me I had to do the will of God at all costs. He had a tendency to refer to me as a Backslidden Baptist Preacher. He encouraged me to get the infilling of the Holy Ghost. After being filled and gifted, my life in the Lord was not the same. We had a service every day at his church. Never mind he had a live radio broadcast daily. The only time we didn't have service was when he had to preach at another church.

God used this relationship with him to teach me the importance of getting in and staying in the presence of God. I also learned how not to sow seeds of negativity. I realized the importance of ministering every day. All of the shelters I had gone to had a service every day. Most places would not allow you to stay if you didn't go to chapel services either before or after the feeding.

Most homeless went to the chapel services only because they had to. They had no expectation from the Lord and in most cases didn't pay attention. I thanked God more and more for the lessons he allowed me to learn from this Ministry.

Bishop Carter took me to the store to buy me a suit and some shoes. We went to Atlantic City to a store called Casino Male. He told the salesperson I needed a suit, a white shirt, necktie and pocket square and some fittums. The clerk laughed and responded I might have to kill the cow to fit them. I had no idea he was talking about my feet. He could not believe I wore a size fifteen. He said Stacy Adam had made the Madison in a fifteen and he thought the only color it came in was black, thank God for this blessing!!! This was the second time I didn't have to go to the thrift store to find something to wear.

Now I could finally feel like I belong in the services and feel right at home. I didn't worry about why it took so long I just began to rejoice. I was taken back to Jacksonville in my mind and thought about how there was nothing available at the thrift store for me. Why when given an opportunity to be a blessing we seek the cheapest way out. We have to get out of the leftover mode. Too many times companies donate their spoils and because they get a tax write-off you would think they would give from their first fruits.

I was now a part of the worship service, singing with the choir and every now and then I sang a solo or lead. Bishop told me I needed to call my mother and let her know I was fine. Connie my sister answered the phone because mother was not at home. She confirmed everything I had told Bishop about the old me, as if she was trying to stop what the Lord had in store for me. As with every mentor and leader, the BIBLE says know them that labor among you, what better way to learn about someone than through the family.

Bishop Carter did not settle for that phone conversation so he took me back to my mother's house and they had a good meeting. I decided to go to visit some friends and clear my head about the purpose for the meeting. I went to some of the shelters and hang out spots for the homeless. I was not appropriately dressed; I didn't have a bag so they knew I was not there in a state of homelessness. We had prayer, and then I went to the shelter to see the administrator and the Chaplain.

Because I had a suit on they told me I looked like a preacher. I was asked if I wanted a job on staff. I could not see myself on staff after all I saw when I was there in a state of homelessness. My response was I would pray about it and get back with them. I talked with the chaplain and he thanked me for the meeting we had before his mother died. He had always wondered after that meeting, how I knew his mother was dying. He prayed he would see me again to thank me for the talk.

I had to get back to mothers and get the car back to the Bishop. He felt good, I told him everything and above all I hid nothing. Mother told him what she could about the unsaved son and Connie told him everything else. Bishop told me he thanked God for saving me because I was a mess.

More than anything else I know how we are to look upon the unsaved homeless and try to help them accept the fact God is a loving, forgiving, and merciful God. He is always waiting for them to come clean about all of their sins. He has a plan for their lives and He will order their steps to allow his plan to come to pass. It begins with confessing that they need more than physical help and seeking spiritual help.

Because of rules and restrictions some facilities that attended to the homeless could not talk about JESUS. I was not part of that facility I would at times ask for a Bible to read. Some of the homeless would come over and ask questions about the Bible. This would reveal they knew more about the Bible than most people would give them credit.

God gives people an opportunity to minister to the homeless and it is so sad we really don't know how too. We must be lead by the Lord to know how, and what to do. People really don't know what to do to encourage the homeless to change. It is simple but we make it complicated. One has to be called and anointed to work with homeless. They don't need to be told they are homeless because they already know they are homeless and how they became homeless. They need to be helped out of the natural and turned over to the spiritual. They need a personal relationship with the Lord. We need to turn to the Lord for wisdom and compassion in order to be able to help effectively.

How can someone help in the spiritual when they don't know the Spirit? The process begins with us presenting them to God "just as they are" then allowing God to do the changing in them. We are to be light in the midst of darkness. We often fail because we try to help God and we fail to realize we do more damage than good. We don't realize the impact we have on people by our actions.

I went back to the homeless soup kitchen in Atlantic City. Everybody was talking about this church that feed the homeless lunch every day so I went to see what they were talking about.

I meet this lady that fed the homeless from her home for years; somehow she had so many people she fed everyday she would run out of food and seats. Because Miss Jessie was so popular, she needed a larger facility to meet the needs of the guest she had every day. The Church she fed from would receive food donations from the casinos. I was glad I was able to talk to her; I even volunteered to help every day. I was told I would be asked, to pray and bless the food for the homeless. I sang a solo every day.

The guest would go and line up for the first feeding and let other people go in front of them, because they didn't want to be a part of the church service before the feeding. They would have to listen to a message from the volunteer ministers. In most cases the substance they were under the influence of would make them act up so they wanted to wait for the second feeding.

I could not understand why there were so many people every day that were hurting and always living the dream of going to the casino to hit it big. The people that ministered to these people daily were never available to present them to Jesus as broken Vessels that needed healing and deliverance. The beauty of it all is this is a great way to talk to people about Jesus.

When they are hungry they tend not to listen in appreciation to the host. In most cases you would hear the homeless saying they wished they had church after they ate. I find the trust level after they calm down is incredible. They were more attentive also. Of course you know the best way to sober up anyone is to feed them. The ears have a tendency to work better when there are no distractions and the stomach is full.

Let's look at a simple example. A wife and mother want to plan meals for the week and desire to talk to her husband but unlike women men are not supposed to be able to do more than one thing at a time. She begins to put her sexy voice to the grind and she says to him; "honey I need to talk to you." You acknowledge you are ready to listen, but you can't put the paper down, stop watching the game, or get off the internet and give her your undivided attention. When she says I am trying to talk to you after she turns the volume up in her voice you find eye to eye contact and finally say I'm sorry.

We have become a selfish people. If we look at our relationship with God as we do our relationships with our perspective mate it would be totally different. We want to introduce our fiancé to Lottie Dottie and everybody. We can't wait to introduce them to our parents. We are the bride of Christ and we act like we can't introduce Him to others as if we are ashamed of Him.

CHAPTER FOURTEEN

"Whatsoever thy hand findeth to do, do it with thy might; for there is no work, nor device, nor knowledge, nor wisdom, in the grave, whither thou goest."Ecclesiastes 9:10

When we talk about doing something for the homeless we need to really seek God as to how and what to do. If we try to help in our own abilities we could make a mess of things and the help we would offer would be of no effect. Because He lives in us we should depend on Him for guidance and wisdom.

Let us focus on the fisherman for a moment. I have a friend that loves to fish. Many nights he could not sleep because he was going fishing early the next morning, he would be so excited and happy; he was like a kid in a candy store. Well, more like a kid in an electronics store. He had great expectation of catching fish.

Theo told me this story once about how he would get up real early in the morning and be in the water by three or four (in the morning) at least three times a month. He told me about the different bait he would use to try to catch fish. Theo would use all kind of bait; worms, chicken livers, hot dogs, and crickets. Theo would tell me it seems to have made no difference what kind of bait he used he would always return home with fish. Theo went home and his wife asked him what did he catch, his response would be "a cold". She asked; "where did you catch these"? He told her on sale at the market.

He would buy them from the market to make it appear he caught them when his wife knew all the time he purchased them from the market. So she would pray for him to catch something so one day he caught one fish. When he returned home he had put that one fish he caught on top of the fish he brought from the market. When she saw that fish on top she began to praise the Lord for that one fish. He asked, what is wrong with you woman? She replied "you finally caught one, I have seen those other fish you been having in the bucket and I knew they came from the market, the Lord has heard and answered my prayer".

I took the time to tell him his wife was like the angels in heaven rejoicing over on sinner repenting. I wanted to preach a sermon from Luke 15:1-7 and title it **"I Lost My Sheep and I Can't Rest Until I Find Him"**. I didn't. I told him it is like some of the homeless I had been around. I must have talked one on one to hundreds and maybe one percent of them would respond to the invitation to accept Jesus as their Savior. He kept fishing even though he didn't stop fishing he finally caught one.

I have felt the frustration of some of the people that feed the homeless and they would tell me it is hard to help someone that doesn't want to be helped. I would tell them to keep trying and one day someone would respond. It is important to always pray before ministering to the homeless. It is important to ask God to give you the wisdom, love and compassion, not pity to work with them. It is important to pray for the homeless before and after you are used by God to try to reach them. You really want to pray after you minister to the homeless to ask God to protect the seed. Remember some plant, some water, but God gives the increase.

Ok let us move on to another fish story. Well, better put a story about me fishing. I was in Huntington Station, New York after my journey. A friend of mine invited me on a fishing trip after he went to Church with me the Sunday before. After I preached he told me he had a surprise for me for my birthday. He told me he was picking me up at 5:00 am. We went on a fishing boat to go fishing. Just like the other fisherman we went and stayed all day and caught nothing. I really caught a cold. I was not prepared for the cold air coming off the water. Timothy thought I needed to get away and he told me when I had the altar call he wanted to come up for prayer but he didn't want the people to know he had cancer.

Because Timothy had cancer he felt so relaxed when he went fishing and he felt he could really talk to the Lord on the water. Timothy thought it was something special about me praying and he asked God to allow me to pray for him on the water. We prayed and God healed him. We caught no fish but we bought some from the boatman. He was healed but we caught no fish. We caught no fish but he was healed. Let me leave that alone!!! I went fishing for one purpose and God saw Timothy's need and faith and performed a miracle.

Every time I minister to the homeless I see an opportunity for God to perform a miracle in their lives if I introduce them to Him just like they are. Even though Timothy and I didn't catch any fish he got just what he needed from the Lord. I really am glad I didn't catch any fish. I don't believe I was ready for the process of catching or eating the fish. You see I didn't want to get that <u>smell</u> of the fish on my hand or in my clothes.

Well, I am reminded of the work involved in getting to eat the fish you catch. First you have to bait the line to catch the fish. When you catch him or her you have to take that stinking fish off the line. Then you have to preserve it until you can clean it, dress it, cook it and give thanks before you eat. It is cheaper and easier to go to a restaurant and order the fish and let them cook it for you.

CHAPTER FIFTEEN

"For the poor shall never cease out of the land: therefore I command thee, saying, Thou shalt open thine hand wide unto thy brother, to thy poor, and to thy needy, in thy land." Deuteronomy 15:11

We don't have to only reach out to them on Thanksgiving and Christmas. Of course we as parents have to teach our children to be grateful and appreciative for what they have. I could not understand how by taking them to a soup kitchen on Thanksgiving and Christmas to volunteer to feed the homeless accomplish that.

What would you do when your child tells you they really enjoyed going to the shelter and volunteering to feed the homeless?

- Can we go every week?
- Can I give them a hug?
- Can I mingle and talk to them?
- How did these people get like that?
- Why are there so many homeless people?
- Why do they smell so bad?

I have heard these questions and the answer most times would be; shush! Don't talk so loud one of them might hear you. We will talk about it when we get home.

Let us look at after Thanksgiving and Christmas

with some ideas I have been pondering in my mind. Well, after Christmas we have New Years, wow, Christmas has not had a chance to wear off yet you go out of your way to speak a word over some homeless person's life, and we kill them in our very next statement. They will always be a bum or they will never change. OOPS!!! I know I am not talking about you!!! I'm talking about what I heard many times.

Okay we have the super bowl!!! Most Americans look forward to the super bowl and their favorite teams playing or they choose a team of the division that is the same as their favorite team. Both teams have players that are Christians; men of faith; and want to win. There is only one winner. People celebrate the pre super bowl with cook outs everywhere. They eat with folk they have never seen before while waiting for the kick off. The countdown for the game is more than for the lift off from the space station you know t-minus... Most homeless don't have the ability to see the game and will have to wait until the next day to find out who won.

Well, we have Valentine's Day a holiday of love. What better way to show love to the homeless even if it is the next day. Most stores have closeout sales on candy late at night and the very next day. Wow I could see that homeless persons face when they get candy at the shelter and some would respond with "somebody really loves us".

Well, March is a good time to focus on not only

spring, but change. It is a divine opportunity to go downtown in your area to mingle with the homeless. They always hang around the shelter, the parks, the library, and bus stations. When we take the opportunity to introduce them to Jesus and help them to understand Jesus loves them it will be like a wild fire moving upon this land to promote change in their lives.

April is a month I want to skip because I never have liked April 1. May is the month so many homeless women have a serious time with depression and feel they have failed their kids. There are also skeletons in their closet about the way their mothers treated them when they were coming up or when they made mistakes they have to be reminded of everyday.

Most homeless men can't look themselves in the mirror when father's day rolls around especially when they have multiple baby mommas. They always talked about I wish I had been a better father and I pray my son don't end up like me.

You can be creative in finding something to do for the rest of the months but we must remember there is no need of reminding them or asking ourselves how they became homeless. We need to find a life line, raft, float or become a life guard in their lives. We need not have pity on them but genuine compassion. Trust me the homeless will try anything to get you to do something to help, always use wisdom and as often as you can have a witness when you try to help.

I pray you have enjoyed the trip and it has been a blessing to you as I was truly blessed to have been educated as to how the homeless are dealt with on the east coast in the areas I went. Now it's time to take the initiative to seek the Lord as to how you can be a blessing in ministering to the homeless, whether it's through a word, a kind deed or simply prayer. Your support is needed in this day and time and the works that you do as a representative of Christ has eternal value.

In the words of the Master *"When the Son of man shall come in his glory, and all the holy angels with him, then shall he sit upon the throne of his glory: And before him shall be gathered all nations: and he shall separate them one from another, as a shepherd divideth his sheep from the goats: And he shall set the sheep on his right hand, but the goats on the left. Then shall the King say unto them on his right hand, Come, ye blessed of my Father, inherit the kingdom prepared for you from the foundation of the world: For I was an hungred, and ye gave me meat: I was thirsty, and ye gave me drink: I was a stranger, and ye took me in: Naked, and ye clothed me: I was sick, and ye visited me: I was in prison, and ye came unto me. Then shall the righteous answer him, saying, Lord, when saw we thee an hungred, and fed thee? or thirsty, and gave thee drink? When saw we thee a stranger, and took thee in? or naked, and clothed thee? Or when saw we thee sick, or in prison, and came unto thee? And the King shall answer and say unto them, Verily I say unto you, Inasmuch as ye have done it unto one of the least of these my brethren, ye have done it unto me.*

Then shall he say also unto them on the left hand, Depart from me, ye cursed, into everlasting fire, prepared for the devil and his angels: For I was an hungred, and ye gave me no meat: I was thirsty, and ye gave me no drink: I was a stranger, and ye took me not in: naked, and ye clothed me not: sick, and in prison, and ye visited me not. Then shall they also answer him, saying, Lord, when saw we thee an hungred, or athirst, or a stranger, or naked, or sick, or in prison, and did not minister unto thee? Then shall he answer them, saying, Verily I say unto you, Inasmuch as ye did it not to one of the least of these, ye did it not to me. And these shall go away into everlasting punishment: but the righteous into life eternal. Matthew 25:31-46

CHAPTER SIXTEEN

Pastor Anita Flores-Bryant
Joining the journey of Faith

I know Lord. You asked me to write my experiences and I have been procrastinating. Maybe because I'm scared of what may come out. Like today I'm a roller coaster of emotions, I have been through so much, but I'm not complaining.

I'm a better person, I'm stronger, and I feel like I can face anything. First because my faith and trust in you my Lord has grown so much throughout this journey that I cannot explain it. It is like when you take a little child and you sit them on top of the refrigerator and you open your arms and tell the child to jump and the child does not hesitate and jumps into your arms. That's me right now. It does not matter how hard it seems if you tell me do it, it is done. Thank you Jesus.

I had no idea that the process for my faith to get to this level would take a little over seven years. In April of 2004 I was asked by my mother to come and stay with her for a few weeks, my family was concerned because I had come out of a real bad marriage of 14 years and allowed myself to be fooled by two men that called themselves to be men of God and one of them tricked me into marrying him and a year later the little money I had was gone and that marriage was not valid. I was not legally married.

Well this threw me into an almost suicidal depression. So I agreed to go to New York with my mom. After two weeks I agreed to stay with her and find a job, slowly I was getting back on my feet and feeling much better. I had decided I will never get married again and I would just devote myself to serving the Lord. At the end of October of the same year, on a Sunday afternoon my mother wanted us to go to church a little early so that we could pray for a little while before the church service, I love praying so I agreed and we went.

When we got to church at the basement of the church, there were two Godly men there, my mom knew them both. One of them was Bishop Bryant, the prophet my mom had been talking to me about for the past three years and every time I would visit her I would miss meeting him. We talked and prayed and we all went our separate ways, but about a month later my phone rings and it's Bishop Bryant, telling me he had something important to tell me from the Lord, I was driving so I pulled over and listened to what he had to say. He told me that three years ago the Lord spoke to him and told him I was going to be his wife. He was molding and shaping me for him and even gave him my name. I was speechless and upset, I told him I was sorry but there was no way this was going to happen, I had made a decision to never marry again and the Lord knew it. He told me it was ok he was going to continue praying.

Well for the next three days I walked around in

shock, I remember people asking me if anything was wrong because I was not myself. I will never forget how I felt, I was scared and confused. I was scared because I was afraid of being tricked again; I was scared because I had made a promise to the Lord of serving Him the rest of my life and doing whatever he asked of me. So my mind was going a hundred miles an hour, I could not trust anyone with this information, especially my family. They would commit me to a mental institution and throw away the key. After the third day I considered to at least try and find out if this was God's will. So I called two Godly friends and I told them both. I am not going to give you details, but I need you to fast and pray for a decision that I need to make. I told them that a Godly man told me I was going to be his wife.

About two months later one of my friends called me and asked me to come to her house the following weekend to fast and pray to receive an answer from God. I went and had an awesome experience with the Lord. Well to my surprise, the day I was going home the Lord spoke thru my friend and even gave me my husband's full name and details about our future relationship and ministry. To me this was overwhelming; no one had ever spoken to me like that. More shocking was that my friend did not speak English and she pronounced his name perfectly. Well that same week I called my other friend, a Pastor from where I am from, Costa Rica. He told me do not fear. He is your husband and he described him to a "t". Wow here I go again on a roller coaster of emotions. So I had more praying to do. See while I waited for an answer we were talking on the phone, I was trying to at least be his friend, and anytime he would call me baby, I use to get mad and tell him "I am not your baby". I thank God for his patience. So I prayed and told God, I will summit to your will, but you need to help me to see him the way you see him, and love him the way you love him, because I can't. Now don't ask me how and when it happened but it did, seven years later I love him more than my life. I thank God for him every day.

That was the beginning of my journey. My husband as you already have read was already on his journey and now I was joining him. We were obeying God but against the world. Why against the world? Well, I'm Hispanic, clear skin so I may look white, and he is Black. The Lord told us that our relationship was going to help destroy the prejudice in the church. I worked, he lived by faith. In my new journey I was to leave everything behind. At the end of September in 2005 the Lord told me October 15 not before not after. So October 15, 2005 we got married, I quit my job and the Lord told us to go to Jacksonville Fla.

We got our little belongings and the little money we had and on the road we went. We did not go right away. We were in N.Y. for a month and a few days, I learned what it was like to make a living by selling scrap metal or pallets. I had never imagined that this was possible. We made enough money to pay a hotel room and eat. Some days making enough for that day, wow, then the Lord would throw a curve ball, like we be in the hotel getting ready for a new day and he would say "do not go anywhere today", what?, are you kidding?, no, this is what He said. Ok, I would go back to bed, waiting for the desk clerk to call and say are you paying for another day? Or are you leaving? And then the phone rings and it is someone telling us, the Lord told me to bless you. Where are you? I need to send you a western union, and it would be enough for 3 or 4 days in the hotel, gas and food.

See up to that time, I had faith, my parents had taught me to trust the Lord to make a way, to heal and to provide etc… But I did not know the meaning of faith. Not true faith, where you tell the Lord I trust in you completely. The Lord was teaching me a whole new meaning of faith, wow.

Another thing happened while I was beginning my journey, my life style changed, I could not get my nails and hair done again, I was losing touch with my friends, I had lost touch with my family and according to them I had brought shame to the family. They did not want to know anything from me and if they did it was not sincere. I also lost my friends because I was ashamed to tell them what I was doing, not that I got married but how much my life was changing. I did not want to answer their questions; I had been through too much.

Now through all this I'm already a Pastor, I was raised in church, my dad was a pastor, so I think I know a lot, and I'm beginning to deal with skeletons I did not know were in my closet. I'm telling this because God has asked me to write my experiences, and seven years later he is bringing things to me I did not remember or I just wanted to forget.

I was not totally healed from all of my wounds from my childhood into adulthood. Through this the first skeleton comes out and I began drinking, it was wine, sometimes beer. I was drinking there is no excuses but it was a way to escape. I was not getting drunk every day but I did find myself drinking more each day. Then the guilt came because I know better, I should not do this, where am I going to go if I die, I am a Pastor, etc...

Where is my husband, in all this? Well being the Godly man that he is, he was praying, and loving me through it. He had his own instructions from God. His faith level was way above mine. Today I know this lesson was mainly for me. I was flunking big time, because at this time I was fighting with my husband, questioning, telling him, I'm going to get a job, well you can imagine what a person in my situation would do or say. So after more than a month in this mess, he sees a friend that knows his painting and carpenter skills and tells him he has a friend in Pennsylvania, that needs some work done in his house, well we were on our way to Fl. So off we went, the man wanted his basement done and two and a half months later we are house slaves. What am I talking about?

Yes house slaves, he was not giving my husband any money for the work and I was cleaning and babysitting for free. Oh My God, what is this? Well it was a week before Valentine's Day and I told the man to get the material needed and let my husband finish the basement because on February 14 whether he is done or not we are out of here. He had not paid us any money up to this time. But God was teaching me about faith and trust and I already told God I do not know how you are going to do it but you have to get us out of here.

Well the day after I told the man that, my daughter called me and said, mom give me your address I want to send you some money so you and your husband can go have a valentine's dinner. I did and to my surprised she sent me three hundred dollars, wow. I cried, I did not know what to say, but I knew I was out. The man left out of town for four days and my husband and I worked day and night and we got his basement done that Sunday. That weekend it snowed a lot but on Monday, God did something crazy with the weather, the temperature went up in the high sixties. We were able to redo our load, pack and get the blazer ready and Tuesday morning was also Valentine's Day and we were saying goodbye. For me it was the best day ever because we were out of there. At this point the young man was looking at us funny; he had a wicked smile on him. You see he had not paid us and had no intentions of paying us, he had more work he wanted done and because we had been in his house for over two months and he was giving us just a little money and a little food. When we first came to his house we had agreed that if he gave us food and shelter, my husband was not going to charge him the rate that the work was going for.

He had a freezer with meat and he told me to take meat from there to cook and it was all chicken, he was Muslim and he did not want any type of pork cooked in his house. It was not a problem for us because we both loved chicken but the last month we were there he cut everything off, he would order out for him and his family and would not include his mother and her boyfriend who were also living there. I felt bad and would cook enough for all of us. I would pray and ask God to give me ideas, because there was hardly anything to season with. One day he came in and actually got upset and asked me where I got gourmet food from, I laughed and told him to come and look it was chicken.

With no money where was I going to get gourmet food from? His mother loved it, she would tell me, Miss Anita, I don't know how you do it but this is delicious. God was teaching me to do a lot with little and how to rejoice and not complain. Well the day came for us to go and not look back. He gave us a thick envelope with money, my husband said God said do not open the envelope till we get into New

Jersey and we did. Well Father knows best, a job that was worth at least five thousand dollars, we should have gotten at least two thousand and he gave us eighty nine dollars, all in single bills. " Jesus, have mercy".

Yes we were angry but we did not look back, like Lot did, we did not look back; I still do not know how we made it to Jacksonville, Fla. His intentions were for us to have to return to his house, so we heard from a friend that he was waiting and was sure we would be back. We could not go too far with that money, But God!

We stopped in New Jersey for a couple of days to visit a friend of my husband and we had to leave part of our load at his house to return later for it. We left and I really don't know how we made it to Jacksonville, Fl. But we did and our adventure continued.

I was not totally happy, I had lived in Fla. For thirty something years and did not want to be there, but God had other plans. He was molding and shaping me through all of this, we lived in a hotel for a while, again selling scrap and pallets, then he found a job painting for a contractor. I started helping and began learning how to paint, two of my kids came to live with us, but that did not go well, we were all much wounded, from my previous 14 year marriage. That is a whole different story that I cannot tell right now.

Almost two years later my husband was talking to

a friend from New York that asked us to run a revival in Georgia, we did and then he asked if we could run the church for him, and we moved to Georgia.

I was happy to go and get a new start. I honestly did not like Florida, from the first time I had stepped in it in 1979 it had been nothing but pain and hardship. The only good thing that had come out of there was my 3 children and 3 grandchildren and a few real good friends.

Well I was happy at last and was thinking maybe now we can have a half normal life. Think again, my faith journey continues. We spend almost two months living in the church, no showers, sleeping on the floor, cold winter, no heat, eating sometimes once a day, because his friend was not supporting us, we were not working and there was no offerings, but the church was growing, we were restoring drug addicts, people were changing, it was great. We found another contractor and started to work for him, we left the church because it was impossible to work with the man that owned the church and he wanted things his way not God's way, so we left.

It was going good, we started to see money and we got a place to live. We had food and we started to do daily devotionals at work and a year later our boss fell in love and things started to change. It got to the point that we were back in a hotel room, homeless, for a few days, then we found a house. By then I had my oldest son, my nephew, my grandson a cat and two dogs. We were not alone any more the responsibility was there and bigger, from time to time I found myself struggling with my drinking, sometimes worse than others but guilt was killing me. I had no one to go to and I had no one to trust, I could not make this go away, dear God do something or take me. Every time God gave me a word through someone He would tell me I see your heart and I'm with you, you are going to be ok.

Today I look back and understand that I had wounds in my heart most of all I had unforgiveness, not against others but I had not forgiven myself. My children and I had gone through a lot and I had been in and out of church. I felt I had not been a good parent and if I had made better choices they would have had a better life. Well it took me a while to learn that it was not my fault and that God had forgiven my past, who was I not to accept his forgiveness and forgive myself. Not until I had forgiven myself was I able to overcome and be set free.

I also have learned through this experience that we have a lot of people in church struggling with hiding addictions and with depression and they are both scared and ashamed to tell anyone and get some help. By God allowing me to struggle with this, I develop understanding and compassion and I feel more equipped to help others.

During the time we were Pastoring that church we met a Bishop that later on asked me to help in a women's seminar and then preach at church because he was deathly ill and did not have the strength.

We went with him and it was the beginning of a wonderful new relationship. We ended up staying and helping that Pastor out and he had been asking God for help. My husband and I would take turns preaching, we baptized over 30 people in less than two years, when we left the church had close to a hundred people and everything was great.

Now we are five years into our marriage and we are still going through a lot, but our relationship is growing strong. I was able to reestablish my relationship with my mom and even though we had to move and I took this time to tell my kids and nephew to find a place of their own, things were good. My faith had grown so much, I was beginning to trust God in areas I never knew it was possible. He showed me how sometimes I did not even have to pray for things just think or wish them and it would happen. For example, again we are still living by faith, jobs here and there, but nothing stable. So I had to always make the best of whatever little money we had. It was the beginning of spring and I kept telling my husband I want a tomato plant, next time you have money we are buying one, well every time I would get money I would find other important things and forget the tomato plant, and one morning I'm going down the steps of my kitchen into the back yard and I see this beautiful plant to my left, I yelled for my husband and I asked him when did you plant this tomato plant? His reply was, women are you crazy? I did not plant anything. Well it is a tomato plant we both agree. Long story short, I had the most beautiful tomato plant. I stopped counting tomatoes at 60 and well into late November when the first frost came. Praise my wonderful God for ever.

So at that moment I learned that as long as I was in obedience to God he would supply all my needs or wants. Well we got the notice to vacate that house, no money or place to go. The next day on our way to pay the light bill, we saw a house for sale or rent, my husband said stop that's our house, well I did but even though my faith had grown a lot, it was not yet were his was, any way, that afternoon, no money down we had the house key and the okay to start moving.

At this time, my kids go their own way, my relationship with my mom is renewed and God has stepped in and was doing a new thing in our life. I have never been able to have a good relationship with her but during the five years that we had no contact I had been praying and helping two dear friends with their relationship with their mothers, and God had restored them. Meanwhile I had totally giving up on mine but God had a wonderful surprise for me; five years later we started talking again, at first it was hard for me because I was afraid it was going to happen again. I had to pray and ask God to help me. Two months later we went to Mexico to visit my sister, we came back and she stayed with us for a month it was great.

After coming back from Mexico and after my mom left we came to realize that our time was up in the church we had been for two years. It was really hard for my husband because he had true love for them, I did also but God had totally disconnected me from them.

Financially things were getting really hard and we could not find work, it was becoming harder to pay our bills and the house we were in, we had agreed to paint and restore little by little. However, the landlord wanted us to pay regardless of all the work we had done. In June of 2012 we ended up in court and we lost, we appealed and we lost again.

Remember at the beginning of my writing I was telling you that God had told us that our mixed relationship was going to help destroy the prejudices in the body of Christ. Well we live in Central Ga. a place made out of a lot of little towns that are stuck in tradition and very religious. If anybody tells you that there is no more racism or prejudice in the United States I can tell them it is a lie. I am from Costa Rica, I am Spanish but I was raised in this country and in my 40 something years of living here I have not experienced the things that I have in this place. It is sad and heart breaking because it is mostly coming from people that call themselves Christians or religious.

The first time we experience this was when we came to Montezuma Ga. in 2007, we stopped at one of the 2 hotels there and it was a Days Inn. My husband went to the counter and asked if they had a room and he was told yes, I came in and put my arm around my husband's arm the desk clerk looked at us funny and said he had made a mistake they had a big convention coming and all the rooms were filled. We walked out and we ran into this real friendly Afro-American guy and my husband asked him if he could go in there and ask for a room. The man did, and the clerk said yes we do, how many days would you need it for. We were blown away. There was no place in the Inn for us. Wow! I kind of understand now how Mary and Joseph felt.

A few weeks later my husband is standing outside the church and this man stopped his car and said to him I have some advice for you, if you don't want anything to happen to you or that white lady of yours you need to leave town. Take her somewhere deep in the woods if you want to stay. I could not believe this, it scared me, and I was ready to go, oh my God! What are we doing in this place?

Well this was the beginning of many more experiences from people looking at us funny to people not even wanting to shake my hand at church. So at this time I am not going to a church I have gotten tired of being judged or looked at funny. So unless there is an engagement I stay home. See, like I told my husband if not going to church is a sin I rather sin by myself. When I go to church and people are judging me I feel I am making them sin for judging and I am sinning because I see thru them and I get upset. Now my husband is a highly anointed man of God and it is sad that he cannot get preaching engagements. He has been told by others that the main reason is because of me. I really thank God for the love we both have for each other and we both have for the Lord. Because it makes you feel like just walking away from it all. But God has been good, we found out about a prayer line that is on twice a day every day of the week (4:45 am and 7:00 pm) holidays included, we have joined and we have been greatly blessed by it, God has been using it to bless us and we have also had the opportunity to preach and bless others. I honestly look forward to it every day. I am the only Spanish person on it but I feel loved and I am looking forward to meeting these people in person real soon.

Now 10/15/2012 we have been married for seven years and we have been in Georgia for about five years. You would think that we would be nice and settled` here but we are not, it feels worse than when we first got here. I know and understand that it was an assignment and part of our molding and shaping, but my Lord please give me some strength.

Today is our wedding anniversary and our lights got cut off. It's been about a month that my husband has been feeling sick, he has not been himself and a few days ago he woke up with his right side of his face swollen and in pain. As the days are going by it seem to be getting worse. So he went to a hospital nearby and was told that he has a real bad case of sinuses. He is 60 yrs old and has never had any problems with his sinuses. He was given antibiotics, 3 days later he has a big bump under his eye and it was shutting his eye. I got really upset and he did not want to go back to the hospital, he wanted to let the antibiotics work. Well I asked him to go out with me and once I had him in the vehicle I decided on taking him to another hospital that was about 45 minutes away. Thank God I did, the doctor didn't even want to touch him and sent us to a specialist and the next day he was having surgery. He had staph infection and it was on its way to his brain. Thank you Jesus; well he was put on heavy duty antibiotics for 35 days. Well by now because he has not been able to work for two months we are sitting at home with no lights, no running water, car insurance and tag canceled.

But God, this morning we got a phone call from a prophet who began to tell us what we are going thru and why. It was sad to hear that there are still people out there including family members that do not want us together and even hate us. Come on people, really? It's 7 years, don't they know that what God puts together no man or devil can pull apart. Well he wants us praying for mercy because it is not going to be nice. But He is going to bless us and we will get out of this mess. He also told us to pray because he had assigned different people to bless and they were not obeying.

I never saw myself without lights for a whole month. Today is over a month and unless God steps in with a miracle I have no idea when it will happen. I continue to praise Him and rejoice. It does no good to ask questions, I have done that. I have asked why? Are we doing something wrong? Are we in disobedience? Many times obedience will look like disobedience. Everything around you will look like turmoil and chaos. Nothing looks right and you will always have people around you asking questions, making suggestions, judging you and your situation, if you are not careful you will quickly take a step out of the will of God.

Well through all this looking back, I have learned to depend on God. I have learned that I have two choices one is to please God or please people. Guess what, you can never please people and since I have committed to serve and obey God I rather please Him. If I want to obey I must do what He tells me to do and let Him worry about those people that disagree with my life style. It has not been easy lately I have days that are very hard and if I am not careful I can fall back into depression and I refuse to get on that boat again. It is now Thanksgiving Day, no lights, no way to bake a turkey, no invitation to go anywhere; it's just us two and the Lord. So I decided I was not going to get upset or sad, I asked my husband to get me all the boxes marked Christmas that were in the garage. At first he looked at me a little crazy but he went for it. Well I said to him the devil is not going to steal our joy or our holiday spirit from us. So that day I put my tree and Christmas decorations up, I had a blast. I sat down and looked at my husband and said, my faith says I will light up my tree. Praise the Lord.

Well a week later we got a phone call from a friend late at night. He told us to have our banking information ready the next day, because the Lord had told him to put $500.00 in our account. I could not help myself; I cried praising and thanking God. The next day I called the light company because I was short $35.00 and I asked if they would agree to receive $470 and the rest at a later day. After being put on hold for a little bit, I was told yes, but the offer was good only for that day and my lights would be on sometime the next day which was a Saturday, I agreed. Our friend came thru and by 6pm that Friday my light bill had been paid. The next day about 11 am the man showed up to connect the lights and told my husband you were the last one on my list but God made me come and connect yours first, wow, what a God we serve. Praise Him.

That Friday night we had a hot service on the prayer line, it was awesome and I had received a re-charge from the Holy Spirit. Well the next week we started to receive blessing from different areas and we slowly started getting the rest of the bills paid. Praise the Lord.

We were on the prayer line and the Lord told us that real soon we will be packing to get out of here.

Since last year we have been praying and asking God to let us get out of the state of Georgia since He had told us that our assignment here was done. So that was another answered prayer. A few days later I told my husband that I felt in my heart that he was not to try to get any more jobs for the rest of the year and to just concentrate on finishing this book. The next day he was given the same word and a day later we found a publisher and the same night on the prayer line the Lord gave us the final confirmation that the book was to be finished now. This was the time and not to worry because He was going to supply all that we needed. Well my little heart felt like it could not take all this good news at once.

But praise the Lord for the journey it has changed me so much and I know that I am a better person. With a heart of love and compassion to help others, I pray that this book will bless you and teach you that it pays to obey God. Don't forget do you please God or people? You cannot please them both. But I can tell you with all honesty it pays to please God.

Contact Information:

Bishop W.L. Bryant
Phone: 631-629-5952
Email: bishopwlbryant@yahoo.com
anilighthouse@hotmail.com
www.neartotheheartofgod.org

Made in the USA
Middletown, DE
11 March 2022